ADVANCE PRAISE FOR

IN THE **Name** OF **Morality**

"Incisive, comprehensive, definitive, this book makes clear that 'moral education' in the United States, like its Chinese counterpart, is about absolutism, authoritarianism, and dogmatism, not morality or education. Yu's impressive cross-cultural and historical analysis demonstrates that any 'moral decline' in the United States is located on the political right."
—William F. Pinar, St. Bernard Parish Alumni Endowed Professor, Louisiana State University

"*In the Name of Morality: Character Education and Political Control* could not be a more timely or important book. Yu excavates and critiques the political agendas that gird the growing character education movement. In particular, Yu exposes the often bipartisan effort to foreground individual morality over and above a sustained and thoughtful reflection on the social and cultural contexts in which and through which young people live their lives today. Yu's scope of vision, wide range of source material, clear writing, and continual willingness to challenge the seemingly commonsense notions about morality make this an ideal text for undergraduate and graduate students alike. I love this book."
—Greg Dimitriadis, Assistant Professor of Social Foundations of Education, State University of New York at Buffalo

IN THE Name OF Morality

AC / SS Adolescent Cultures, School & Society

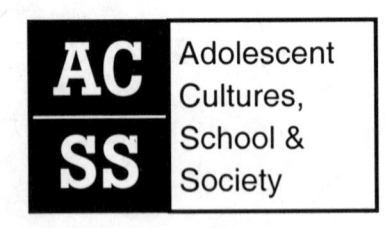

Joseph L. DeVitis & Linda Irwin-DeVitis
GENERAL EDITORS

Vol. 26

PETER LANG
New York • Washington, D.C./Baltimore • Bern
Frankfurt am Main • Berlin • Brussels • Vienna • Oxford

TIANLONG YU

IN THE **Name**
OF **Morality**

Character Education
and Political Control

PETER LANG
New York • Washington, D.C./Baltimore • Bern
Frankfurt am Main • Berlin • Brussels • Vienna • Oxford

Library of Congress Cataloging-in-Publication Data

Yu, Tianlong.
In the name of morality: character education
and political control / Tianlong Yu.
p. cm. — (Adolescent cultures, school, and society; v. 26.)
Includes bibliographical references and index.
1. Moral education—United States. 2. Character. 3. Students—
United States—Conduct of life. I. Title.
II. Series: Adolescent cultures, school & society; v. 26.
LC268.Y83   370.11'4—dc22   2003027184
ISBN 0-8204-6725-1
ISSN 1091-1464

Bibliographic information published by **Die Deutsche Bibliothek**.
Die Deutsche Bibliothek lists this publication in the "Deutsche
Nationalbibliografie"; detailed bibliographic data is available
on the Internet at http://dnb.ddb.de/.

Cover design by Lisa Barfield

The paper in this book meets the guidelines for permanence and durability
of the Committee on Production Guidelines for Book Longevity
of the Council of Library Resources.

© 2004 Peter Lang Publishing, Inc., New York
275 Seventh Avenue, 28th Floor, New York, NY 10001
www.peterlangusa.com

All rights reserved.
Reprint or reproduction, even partially, in all forms such as microfilm,
xerography, microfiche, microcard, and offset strictly prohibited.

Printed in the United States of America

To Lihua,
with love and appreciation

Contents

Foreword by Nel Noddings..ix

Acknowledgments..xi

Introduction..1

1 Ideology, Politics, and Moral Education: A Cross-Cultural Inquiry.......7

2 The Early Character Education Movement: A Historical Perspective...27

3 Moral Decline and the Politicization of Character Education............55

4 Character Education in Theory: Moral Philosophies and Ideologies...103

5 Character Education in Practice: Linkages to Ideologies.................129

6 Back to the Future: Alternative Moral Education
   and School Reform..149

References..157

Index..165

Foreword

Tianlong Yu has provided us with a comprehensive, comparative, and fascinating critique of character education. Using his firsthand knowledge of character education in China, he shows us that many of the errors we identify so easily in the Chinese-communist program of moral education also exist in the current American program.

Both Chinese and American character education programs emphasize the control of behavior. Assuming that the problems of "moral decline" can be traced to individual character flaws (rather than, say, social conditions), they recommend a pattern of socialization that emphasizes the inculcation of virtues. Their approach gives little, if any, attention to the development of critical thinking, and yet we know that critical or reflective thinking is the main safeguard against a sheep-like submission to socialization.

Professor Yu reminds us of the complexity of moral life and moral education. We might ask the question: Are the virtues always virtuous? With vivid examples contrasting Chinese and American interpretations of the virtues, Yu argues convincingly that the virtues are culturally and contextually defined. When we recognize the contextual nature of the virtues and their exercise, we understand that something deeper lies beneath and supports the virtues. A principle of justice? Shared cultural beliefs? Caring? A sense of community? Religion? Exploring these possibilities should be part of the task of moral education.

This clearly and thoughtfully written book should expand our thinking on moral education. Readers should be stimulated to ask: Is there indeed a "moral decline"? Have we identified and formulated the problem accurately? Have we taken all of its features into account? Have we considered a full array of possible solutions? And have we analyzed those possible solutions to see which are compatible with truly democratic life? As we study these questions and engage in dialogue over them, we will see that the present character education movement has given us answers that are simplistic and perhaps misleading.

Nel Noddings

Acknowledgments

This book results from a personal cross-cultural learning journey from China to the United States. Many teachers, mentors, colleagues, students, and friends have guided, supported, and assisted me during this journey and in the production of this book in particular. Lawrence Stedman, Joseph DeVitis, and Nel Noddings were instrumental in guiding my thinking in the creation of the original draft. E. Wayne Ross, Gladys Jiménez, and Barbara Regenspan provided me with important ideas at various writing stages. Hongyu Wang, Mark Garrison, Brad Porfilio, P. Sheehan McHugh, Robert Fetter, and Chuanbao Tan read various chapters and offered invaluable comments. Thanks to my students at D'Youville College, who are preservice and in-service teachers, for their inspiring thoughts on the topic and for constantly reminding me about the importance of such an analysis. Thanks to Joseph DeVitis and Linda Irwin-DeVitis for giving me the opportunity to contribute to the series they edit and to Christopher Myers, Bernadette Shade, and other staff members at Peter Lang for their professional and friendly service and assistance.

Introduction

The character education movement in the United States has become extremely popular as a result of the support it receives—from the White House to local school boards. Within such a pro-character education environment, counterarguments are perhaps not expected, but they are urgently needed. This book presents a critical analysis that will assist readers in delving into the political and ideological underpinnings of character education.

The book examines character education within its larger sociopolitical context. It deconstructs the well-perceived myth of "moral decline" that has been used to justify character education. During a time when we hear repeatedly of the ghastly episodes of school shootings involving disaffected white adolescents and the equally abhorrent corporate CEO corruption scandals, the discourse of moral decline is fashionable. When all these problems are merely viewed as morally misguided behaviors, character education appears to be a moral and pedagogical imperative.

Although the loss of moral consciousness is indeed deplorable, the sweeping claim of "moral decline" is largely unfounded and misleading. The so-called "moral problems" have profound social, cultural, and political roots and must be addressed in their entirety. Overemphasizing their moral implications and rendering the complex problem as personal moral decay cloaks the social nature of the problems, deflects people's attention from their root causes, and leads to poor policy choices and unsuccessful problem-solving efforts.

A look at the past helps us to better understand the present. As David Purpel (1999) comments on the current character education movement: "...this movement, far from being innovative and reforming, represents a long-standing tradition of using schools as agents of social stability, political stasis, and cultural preservation" (p. 83). My historical study of character education in U.S. schools reveals that, especially when American society entered a transition period and the ruling class faced challenges (e.g., during the beginning of the twentieth century and the late 1980s), character education was called upon to solve social problems and socialize people, especially the young, to the established political, economic, and social orders. The emphasis on personal morality thus becomes a subterfuge and aims to maintain the dominant social positions of those in power. To ensure that their privileges are guaranteed and that they will continue to have control over others, the power elites laud their own moral standing and label others as morally inferior. In the name of morality, character education becomes a pedagogy of political control.

Character education is politically charged from its origin; however, character educators attempt to depoliticize it in both theory and practice. Theorists declare that the question "Whose values?" is "distracting" and it has been "settled" (Damon, 2002, p. xiv). Character education is thus said to focus on the so-called "universal virtues" and avoids any politically charged issues. Following their leaders, some teachers argue that hanging posters with uplifting moral messages in school hallways does not demonstrate political conspiracy; a little moralizing about respect and responsibility also does not cause much harm even though it indeed fails to really affect kids' morality.

These depoliticizing claims are at best naïve and at worst deceptive. They should be subject to close examination. Character education follows the tradition of virtue ethics with its Aristotelian root as character educators emphasize values, such as respect and courage, as timeless and universal. They refer admiringly to Aristotle, who promoted the direct teaching of these so-called virtues. However, they ignore the fact that only the metaphysical forms of the so-called virtues may remain unchanged over time, while the substance and nature of each and every virtue have always been socially constructed. Even in Aristotle's era virtues were defined within a unique sociopolitical context and used to discipline people and maintain a rigid social hierarchy. We must remember, virtues have their utilities: They serve interests. The construction of virtues is always tied to privilege, power, and control.

While focusing on teaching "universal virtues" and engaging in community-based decision-making, character educators today ignore important issues of gender, race, class, religion, and culture that decidedly affect the individual's moral life. Character educators are outspoken, famously, in objecting to moral relativism; however, in the name of absolute moral principles, they also define virtues based on particular ideologies and offer relative recommendations to students. A closer look at the character education proposals of Edward Wynne (1989a, 1989b) and Thomas Lickona (1999) reveals the embedded conservatism of Judeo-Christian religious influences. Character educators indeed object to moral relativism because they deny the claim that anyone's values could be equally valid or legitimate; they assume their values are common or universal, representing absolute truths.

While challenging the universality justifications for character education and recognizing that a progressive construction of moral values can avoid the usual philosophical debate about moral absolutism vs. moral relativism, this book places more emphasis on the inconsistencies in character educators' arguments regarding this issue, and shows how "universal values" are actually based upon particular social interests. It is not a matter of whether or not there are absolute moral truths but how the claims of moral truths are relative to the social position of the holder of such claims. One must analyze why the character education leaders have to insist that their particular values are universal. Historically, there has seemed to be an inherent contradiction between U.S. political figures' rhetoric on character education and their advocacy of militarism, from Theodore Roosevelt and Woodrow Wilson to the current time. The last four presidential administrations (Reagan, Bush, Clinton, and Bush) have strongly supported character education at home while embarking on projections of military power abroad. The military actions have often been justified in the name of spreading universal values, namely, democracy and freedom as defined by the U.S. government. This seems to reflect the political leaders' theory of governance, or control, in general, as they believe they have a license to scour the earth as they see fit.

The question of "Whose values?" is not settled yet. As long as there are contending class interests in the society, as long as racism and social inequality affect people's lives, the question of "Whose values?" takes on the utmost importance. Stopping this inquiry inevitably rejects the complexity of the moral life and denies the political nature of character education. Character education, along with any other educational reforms, must be examined within a larger political framework. Teachers must be aware of the ideological orientations of any moral education efforts in schools and recognize the nature of the politicization they might reinforce (unconsciously perhaps) through character education programs. Actually, a good question to ask many dedicated character educators is whether or not what they are doing is truly character building. In so many schools character education is nothing more than behavioral training to maintain an orderly environment, one that directs students to obediently accomplish tasks imposed upon them by governmental officials, large-scale corporations, and other dominant social groups. One example of this form of schoolwork is standardized testing. We must ask, along with this line of work and training, what ideologies are being promoted?

More political and ideological critiques of character education are needed. Such analyses will provide insight on how we view education in a moral way and how we engage in the education of moral people. The political critique of character education here is addressed within a larger search for an alternative moral education curriculum (albeit this search is not the focus of this book) and for an overall educational system that lives up to moral ideals. The most serious problem in contemporary school reform is a moral one, but it is defined differently than character educators. Forced into a uniform, standard curriculum and judged according to standardized tests, students are denied their right to a well-rounded education that necessarily addresses their moral development. The top-down and one-size-fits-all educational approach also ignores the issues of cultural diversity, social justice, and educational equality, issues that need to be seriously addressed if we are ever to construct a moral educational system in America.

Character educators in schools do make an important contribution when they emphasize the moral nature of teaching and schooling, but unfortunately their commitment is unlikely to have much value in a misguided practice. With its inherent perils, character education does not challenge the academic and test-driven reform agenda; instead, it has joined the standards movement and contributed to the oppressive force undermining students' moral well-being. The leaders of the movement, such as William Bennett, Edward Wynne, and Thomas Lickona, all support the overall school reform movement that continues to be content oriented and standards based. As practiced in schools, character education generally means teaching virtues defined in accordance with behavioral objectives thought to enhance academic achievement.

Character education does not represent an encouraging direction for school reform. The overall reform agenda does not challenge the fundamental school structure and value system based on the larger capitalist political, economic, and social hierarchy; therefore it cannot bring significant and positive change to American education. Character education that promotes the cultural politics of conservative power elites only reinforces the status quo and steers school reform in the wrong direction. As transformative school reform is needed, alternative moral education is required.

Introduction

As I said earlier, the search for an alternative moral education approach is not an important task of this book. We must remain cautious when talking about any "alternative" ideas. In accordance with the central question raised in this entire book to character educators, we have to ask ourselves: By whose values do we make choices to create another new model of moral education? That being said, the discussion on alternative moral education will remain brief, eclectic, and open-ended.

An alternative moral education approach, first, must reject the inculcation of virtues. Virtue-centered education is unlikely to produce virtuous people. Character building does not stop at the recitation of context-free moral traits or codes. Moral education is more than what is provided in the prevailing one-virtue-per-month model. Moral education must be mainly concerned with creating a condition and a process in which the moral life can flourish. Such a context-based and process-oriented moral education does not arise from an add-on program but starts with the restructuring of schools. We as educators have a responsibility to challenge many of the established and emerging school practices, such as differential tracking, excessive standardized testing, and impersonal zero-tolerance policies. These practices are, first and foremost, morally deplorable. Equally important, educators must become "cultural workers" (Giroux, 1992) and tackle the problems prevalent in the wider society such as racism, sexism, and classism. We must focus on making the entire school structure, school culture, and educational process morally justifiable and defendable. If we have a moral school where children's morality and character are adequately nurtured and fostered, why do we still need a separate movement or program in moral education?

To address the above issues, the book consists of six chapters. Chapter 1 opens with a cross-cultural inquiry into the complex and crucial relationships among ideology, politics, and moral education and addresses political concerns about the character education movement in the United States from an international perspective. Drawing upon a personal journey, the chapter explores the often-ignored resemblances between China and the United States in moral/character education efforts. While examining the political control in Chinese moral education, the chapter urges a need to demythologize the popular concept of character education in the United States and to challenge its inherent political and ideological orientations.

Chapter 2 addresses character education in its historical context and provides a historical perspective for an examination of the current character education movement. Character education programs in U.S. schools in the early twentieth century are investigated. The purpose and methods of character education as well as its social background and ideological forces are explored.

Chapter 3 brings the study back to today and examines the social and political background of the modern movement. This chapter deconstructs the conception of moral decline in contemporary America promoted by character education leaders and discusses how the claim of moral decline has politicized character education. It analyzes how character education proponents define social and cultural problems as moral problems and urge character education as a remedy. The social and cultural roots of problems among youth, such as violence and drug abuse, are examined. The analysis reveals the political purposes embedded in the call for character education.

Chapter 4 focuses on the theoretical claims of prominent contemporary advocates of character education, such as William Bennett, William Kilpatrick, Edward Wynne, Thomas Lickona, and Kevin Ryan, and examines the ideologies shaping their theories. The chapter explores the philosophical claims of character education to be a virtue-centered approach to moral education and reveals its ideological underpinnings.

Chapter 5 continues the political and ideological analysis of character education by investigating its practice. The chapter critically reviews a number of representative character education curricula, discusses their common pedagogical features, and reveals the ideologies shaping the curriculum and instruction.

Chapter 6 summarizes the major research findings in this study, discusses ideas about building alternative progressive approaches to character education, and addresses issues for future research.

The analyses in these chapters aim to assist readers in identifying the social interests, power relations, and political and sociocultural ideologies that shape the character education movement in the United States. It is my hope that this examination will shed light on the more general issue of moral education and will contribute to our understanding of the moral and political nature of schooling. By deconstructing the character education rationales and practices, the book envisages the empowerment of schools to become agents of moral development, social transformation, and human liberation.

CHAPTER ONE

Ideology, Politics, and Moral Education: A Cross-Cultural Inquiry

Beginning in the 1980s, Americans have witnessed a reemergence of character education. As a formal approach among the broadly based efforts to teach about morals and values in schools, character education comes with its own territory. According to Thomas Lickona (1999), a noted figure in the movement: "Character education is the deliberate effort to cultivate virtue. Virtues are objectively good human qualities....To be effective, character education must be comprehensive, intentionally making use of every phase of school life as an opportunity to develop good character" (p. 23).

The movement has increasing support on many fronts, such as local school districts, professional organizations, and state and federal governments. Former President William Jefferson Clinton declared his support for character education in his 1997 State of the Union Address: "Character education must be taught in our schools. We must teach our children to be good citizens." President George W. Bush is even more enthusiastic about character education than his predecessor. His call for character education is an important part of his overall education reform agenda, which also includes his pronounced support for local control, accountability, high-stakes testing, and school vouchers.

In addition to the presidents' endorsements, political support for character education has taken two other forms: legislation and grants. According to Haynes (2000), by October 2000, sixteen states had mandated or encouraged character education through legislation. Thirty-six states and Washington, D.C., had received federal grants to develop character education initiatives. On November 1, 2002, as a new effort to highlight the Bush administration's commitment to character education, First Lady Laura Bush announced that another $16.7 million in character education grants from the U.S. Department of Education would go to five states and thirty-four school districts across the nation.

Character education has also been addressed in terms of standards, the hallmark of the overall national school reform movement. As Nielson (1998) reported, "Forty-eight of the fifty states have completed or are in the process of completing state educational standards which address character education" (p. 9). As a result of all of this advocacy and support, character education is spreading rapidly in schools across the country.

This book provides a critical analysis of the character education movement in the United States. Specifically, it examines the ideologies that shape the movement and reveals its political nature. Ideology, simply defined, is "the body of doctrine or thought that guides an individual, social movement, institution, or group" (*Webster's College Dictionary*, 1991, p. 668). Ideology is often closely tied to politics. As Railton (2000) notes, "An ideology is in the first instance a set of beliefs or values held by individuals or groups, not a set of propositions considered in itself" (p. 117). Thus, whether a belief or value is ideological will depend upon the nature of the explanation by the people who hold it. An ideology serves certain non-epistemic interests, the political needs of a given social group. Ideologies underlie and guide educational ideals, policies, and practices, including those regarding character education.

Compared with ideologies that are usually the covert origins of school practices, politics is, relatively, a more discernible and practical reality in education. The politics of character education can be understood through observation of its decision-making process. A political analysis of character education focuses on how various social groups and individuals promote certain social interests and power relations through character education and exert influences on the movement. The relationships between ideology, politics, and character education, as thus defined, become the central issues explored by this book.

My political and ideological analysis of the character education movement in the United States has evolved through a personal journey. I am a citizen of China where I was born, raised, and educated. For the past six years, I have been in the United States, first as a graduate student of education and then a teacher-educator. Traveling between East and West, I have come to conceptualize and reconceptualize my philosophy of education and my perspective on moral education, in particular. As a result, the political and ideological aspects of moral education became my major research concern.

Ideology, Politics, and Moral Education

In the following pages of this chapter, I shall address a cross-cultural inquiry into the relationships between ideology, politics, and moral education. Drawing upon an observation of and reflection on my personal journey, I provide a rationale for this study. In other words, my political concern about the character education movement in the United States is addressed from an international perspective.

Chinese Moral Education Today: A Familiar Reality

Summer 2000. A journey home after three years in America. The plane was nearing Beijing when the flight staff told passengers that the Great Wall was right underneath. I looked out of the window; yes, it was there, wriggling across the mountains, like a giant dragon. After centuries of wind and rain, the dragon was still there. Although having seen the Great Wall many times before, I was amazed yet again. Like other Chinese, I have also become naturally proud of it, one of the great wonders of the world. With pride, I told a little Chinese American boy next to me about the history of the Great Wall. Two thousand years ago, there was a great emperor in China. For the first time in Chinese history he united the entire country. He was extremely powerful, but he was still afraid that nations in the north would invade his country, so he built the Great Wall to block them out. After him, all emperors continued to maintain the Great Wall.

Obviously fascinated by my story, the little boy suddenly made a comment: "How come? It can't block planes and missiles!" Smiling, although somewhat shocked by his remark, I said, "There were no planes or missiles at that time…but you are right, a wall cannot block everything." Knowing the little boy could not understand, I said to myself: No, the Great Wall actually never blocked any foreign invasion. It only prevented us from moving out into the world.

The Great Wall still serves as a popular metaphor for the Chinese nation today. People are proud of this great ancient construction without questioning its original purpose or its actual effect. It is considered educational. The Ministry of Education of the central government has included the Great Wall as one of the "national educational bases" used for moral education of the young. School children are led regularly to visit the Great Wall to inspire them to take more pride in their country, their ancestors, and their traditions. According to one official from the ministry: "Such practice has proven to be a successful form of patriotic education" (Sun, 2000). However, he did not inform us what criteria he had used to claim it as a "success."

Nevertheless, patriotic education is one of the most important tasks of moral education in Chinese schools today. At the Center for Moral Education Studies, a research center affiliated to the Ministry of Education, I talked with my former colleagues about the most recent policies on school moral education in China. They showed me some newspaper headlines, and President Jiang's "A Speech on Education" and "Key Issues of Moral Education in 2000: Guidelines from the Ministry of Education" attracted my attention immediately. I read the president's speech first, knowing that what the president says will be the basis of what the ministry says and the ministry's policy will mainly clarify and amplify the president's speech. This is how policy is stated and implemented in China.

Jiang (2000) emphasized moral education in his speech as the core of quality education and thus designated its content. He said, "Speaking of quality, ideological and political quality is the most important one. Accordingly, patriotic education, collective education, and socialist education are the souls of our quality education" (p. 1).[1]

The president's speech indeed became the backbone of the subsequent decisions made by the Ministry of Education. Highlights of the ministry's (2000) policies on moral education included strengthening and improving moral education at all levels of schools; carrying out the Communist Party's educational principles completely; setting political education as the priority of moral education; reinforcing patriotism, collectivism, and socialism in curricula; cultivating students' moral virtues, law-abiding consciousness, and civilized behavioral habits; shaping students' scientific worldviews; and building healthy and strong character in youngsters (p. 2).[2]

One may ask whether policy really affects practice. The answer is yes. Unlike the U.S. public school system, which is highly decentralized and characterized by local control, Chinese education is extremely centralized. The Ministry of Education controls the entire system through a national curriculum for all pre-college schools in every subject, including moral education. Therefore, the president's directive and the ministry's guidelines significantly impact individual schools' moral education practices.

I visited a number of schools in several provinces. I found that schools across the country comply with the ministry's policies. However, they primarily stress moral education by following programs that are already in place. For example, many schools continue to use a 1950s framework called

"Five Loves Education," which includes love of our motherland, love of our people, love of science, love of work, and love of socialism. The fifth love used to be "love of public property" but has been replaced by "love of socialism."

In addition to political education, behavioral training is also a major component of moral education. Schools closely observe various behavioral standards such as the "Twenty Behavior Standards for Elementary School Students" and "Forty Behavior Standards for Secondary School Students" issued by the Ministry of Education in the 1970s. I saw posters of these behavioral standards in most of the classrooms I visited. Even the language is similar to what I was familiar with when I was in school. Students must be good children at home, good students in the school, and good citizens in society. In school, they are expected to work hard and follow the rules, get along with fellow students, and be helpful to each other. At home, they are asked to have reverence for their parents, help with housework, and be economical in everyday spending. In society, they are required to obey the law and help maintain public social order. As a former student in China, I have experienced these behavioral standards as rigorously enforced in schools where students are strictly trained to conform their behaviors to the standards. Currently in Chinese schools, political education and behavioral training remain central to the practice of moral education.

Tracing the Path:
Moral Education in a Changing Time and Place

This type of moral education has evolved through an intense history in communist China, and it has been ingrained into my memory. When I was a little boy during the heyday of the communist Cultural Revolution (1966–1976), I attended numerous meetings in my community to study the works of our "greatest" communist leader, Chairman Mao. I can still recall, even feel, the solemn atmosphere enveloping those meetings. I was totally caught up in this atmosphere even though I could not understand anything of Chairman Mao's teachings. I now wonder whether the adults, most of whom were farmers without much formal education, really understood what they studied either since Chairman Mao's works are mostly quite philosophical and difficult readings. Regardless, they indeed looked absolutely absorbed and pious.

I witness a similar piety in many American churches twenty years later. When devout Christians listen to God's teachings in the Bible, they show unquestioning belief and acceptance. For my parents' generation, Chairman Mao was their God. A Christian believer does not need much critical thinking to follow God's precepts nor did those adults in my community who followed Chairman Mao. Perhaps the adults knew that a little boy like me could not possibly understand Mao's difficult works, yet they had no doubt that children could be influenced by the atmosphere, the environment, and even the process of the imposition of Chairman Mao's ideas.

Similarly, in school, teachers led us in reciting quotations from Chairman Mao's works every day, both during one whole class period and before the regular classes began. We were asked to recite fast and accurately. The memorization was quite effective because even now I can recite many quotations from Chairman Mao's works although I did not fully understand the meaning of those words until many years later. Chairman Mao's teachings were hailed as our highest political and behavioral standards. We were taught to listen to his teachings and to be his good children. That was the bulk of my formal moral education in elementary school.

Some American researchers documented this type of moral education in China in the 1970s. Connell (1976) noted that moral education and political education were inseparable in Chinese schools:

> Moral education is concerned with developing selected kinds of character traits and forms of behavior preferred by the educator. The basis for selection, in China and the U.S.S.R, is political....The good person is the one with the right political attitude. To be a good soldier, peasant, worker, or scholar, one must first possess the correct political views. Technical knowledge and proficiency are essential for the efficient performance of one's tasks, but having the right political attitude ensures that one's task is directed toward the right ends and carried out in the right spirit. (p. 31)

The death of Mao in 1976 and the launch of the so-called "Reform and Open Door" policy in 1978 changed the focus of Chinese education. When I was in middle and high school in the early 1980s, for example, we stopped studying Chairman Mao's works. Moral education in schools was no longer emphasized as it had been during the Cultural Revolution. And as the country rapidly moved toward economic modernization, academics became the real priority of school education. The extremely competitive national college entrance examination, which was resumed after the Cultural Revolution, was the focus of schoolwork and drove curriculum and instruction, even at the elementary level. Precollege education largely turned out to be college preparation. While teaching to tests gradually began to dominate the actual core of school education, moral education lost its prior lofty status in schools.

In spite of this shift, moral education continued to be emphasized at philosophical and policy levels as an integral part of school education. As President Jiang declared, it is considered the most important part of a quality education. As a component of the official curriculum, moral education, in the form of political education and behavioral training, is taught as a separate core subject. Even though it receives much less emphasis than other academic courses, it profoundly influences the lives of both teachers and students.

One striking feature of Chinese moral education is its expanded mission. Over the years, the concept of moral education has been greatly broadened as part of a trend toward "overmoralization" of issues. Chinese educators tend to believe that except for the education for children's intellectual and physical development, which are relatively independent curricular entities, all other efforts, such as civic education and psychological education, are the goals and content of moral education. The aim of moral education is to produce good people who will contribute to the society.

Such a broad conception of moral education is rooted in Mao's theory. Fifty years ago, when Mao formulated an educational policy for the new nation, he required schools to give children a well-rounded education. As Mao (1957/1977) said, "Our educational aim is that we should have our students develop morally, intellectually, and physically, and become the cultivated workers with socialist consciousness." Mao's vision not only set a theoretical framework for moral education but also guaranteed the political influence within its practice.

In reality, under this broad umbrella of moral education, there is a tendency to connect social problems to moral issues and use moral education to remedy social ills. After the death of Mao, the country entered a great transition period, facing a series of social upheavals and problems, such as unethical business behavior, crime, and an increasing divorce rate. A strong voice from the government and the government-controlled media asked schools to prevent these problems through the implementation of moral education.

Ideologies of Moral Education:
Communism and Confucianism

The broadened notion of moral education embraces Chinese politics and allows ideological domination of its theory and practice. Communism, or rather, party communism, strictly speaking, is the dominant ideology in Chinese political and cultural arenas. The Communist Party is the "unquestionable" leader and it controls all the schools. "We are the Party's children," a popular slogan during the Cultural Revolution, still reflects today's reality: What students learn is largely determined by the Party through a top-down national curriculum, not by students themselves, their parents, or the local communities. Thus, the curriculum of moral education naturally becomes the home of communist-approved ideologies such as patriotism, collectivism, and socialism. Bai (1998) reveals how the Chinese moral education system has been based on the legitimacy of the political leadership of the Communist Party. Under Mao's regime (1949–1976), the legitimacy of the Party was expressed simply as "Listening to what Chairman Mao says." Now this legitimacy has been developed into a formula: "Patriotism = socialism = Chinese Communist Party = the needs of the country and people" (pp. 525–526).

Values favored by these larger ideologies are emphasized while those conflicting with them are ignored, criticized, or forbidden. As Connell (1976) observed, Chinese schools greatly stressed collective virtues. Behaviors associated with various collectives, such as the school, the community, the Party, and the country, share some basic moral elements, including honesty, selflessness, industriousness, respect, and responsibility. Hence, moral education was required to build a collective nature in children.

This reality still pervades Chinese moral education curricula today despite changes the Chinese society is currently experiencing. A diversity of values is actually developing within the society, and it is profoundly affecting young people. As Yuan and Shen (1998) found through their surveys, today's adolescents tend to prefer values that are related to competence and personal effectiveness. The extremely competitive college entrance examination and other high-stakes tests have greatly contributed to this change. Nevertheless, moral education in schools, both theoretically and practically, still ignores the diversity of values and stresses collective values.

One dominant "new" initiative is the recent reemergence of Chinese moral tradition, which represents a revival of Confucianism, particularly across Chinese education. The movement has also been a response to the

Ideology, Politics, and Moral Education

recent social changes. Leaders of the movement bemoan social problems as signs of moral decline and claim a need to rediscover "the quintessence of Confucian ethics" (Zhan, 1996) to address them. (A very similar rationale is found in the U.S. character education movement.) They strongly believe that a return to Confucian tradition will save young people from bad capitalist influences. They regard it as a crucial strategy for the reform of moral education and are making concerted efforts to bring Confucian ethics back to the classroom. A review of research shows many books and articles on the topic. There also have been several large-scale experimental projects to teach selected Confucian virtues to students.

The movement enjoys popularity on many fronts. Nationalists, anticapitalists, and others who are discontented with the communist monopolization of cultural and educational affairs welcome the initiative. They hope it will become an alternative practice to communist-controlled moral education. It is significant and surprising that the Communist Party and the Ministry of Education have also overtly encouraged and strongly supported this movement.

As a moral philosophy and nontheistic religion, Confucianism dominated the Chinese cultural landscape for thousands of years until 1949. When communists overthrew the old regime, they abandoned Confucianism as the state ideology. And during the Cultural Revolution, Confucianism suffered one of the most severe attacks in history. Communists revolutionized Chinese culture with orthodox Marxism, Leninism, and Maoism and forbade any other ideologies to compete with them. Because of the antireligious nature of communism, communists still object to the religious and spiritual components of Confucianism. Nevertheless, they have begun to accept and encourage it as a moral philosophy.

Communists are seeking cultural support from Confucianism for their own social and educational purposes. They are promoting a special version of Confucianism by emphasizing only certain aspects of it. For example, they stress the relational and communal nature of Confucianism, the Confucian call for proper social ordering and harmonious interpersonal relations, the inculcation of community values, and the criticism of individualism. Under the current social and cultural atmosphere in China, Confucianism has been reformulated not to contradict the communist ideologies but rather to support them. Confucian moral philosophy is now compatible with communism's own collective spirit. In Mao's era, communists only embraced communism and the associated ideologies and disregarded the nation's cultural tradition.

Now communists have realized that it will be beneficial for them to integrate their ideologies into the more profound and pervasive Confucian tradition.

What specific values are taught in this return to Confucian tradition? We see values such as loyalty to one's country, commitment to serving one's people, social responsibility, respect for authority, and self-discipline—values that represent a conservative Confucianism and are consistent with communist ideological frameworks. As China's Open-Door policy has resulted in the emergence of new ideologies and values competing with official communist ideologies, the Chinese Communist Party and its government have repeatedly called for a strengthening of political education and a return to the reinterpreted cultural tradition. Their purpose is clear: Use moral education for political control and maintaining communist social hegemony.

Thus, the politicization of moral education in China has been situated within and supported by a cultural tradition that strongly affirms a specific type of moral education. Contrary to many people's hope, the return of Confucianism does little more than reinforce the collective and conservative nature of moral education shaped by communism. Confucianism now stands side by side with communism and shapes Chinese moral education. As a result, this one framework monopolizes moral education. Moral education has largely become a process of imposition of communist and Confucian ideologies and other moral values endorsed by these ideologies, a process of behavioral training and character building according to the prescribed standards and a process of socialization of youngsters to the established communist power relations.

Chinese researchers are, under the guidance of Confucianism and communism, working to make the existing moral education system more effective. Teachers are busy applying the national curriculum of moral education and all other directives, teaching what the government requires them to teach. Critical voices regarding the fundamental political nature of moral education are rarely heard. This situation remains unchanged.[3]

Let us stop and ask several questions. Why am I writing so much about the Chinese practice in a book about American education? What is the connection between Chinese moral education and American moral education? Are there really any similarities between these two countries in moral education? Jie Lu (2000), a prominent professor of education in China states:

> Chinese moral education still fits in a traditional model, theoretically and practically. The process of moral education is largely a process of imposition of external moral

influences, which are mainly prescribed moral principles and rules. Such a process puts its stress on shaping students' behaviors according to those principles and rules. This is exactly what Kohlberg had criticized: inculcation of values, training of behaviors, a "bag of virtues" approach, and a traditional character education model. (p. 3)[4]

According to this viewpoint, the Chinese approach to moral education largely falls within the same model as character education programs in the United States. We have discussed the political control of Chinese moral education. As Bai (1998) points out, "In the Chinese context, the 'Bag of virtues' has already been 'filtered' by the standards of political preference and blended with political values" (p. 526). Now, let us look at this issue in the United States. Specifically, what are the political and ideological influences in American character education?

Character Education in the United States: Targeting the Political

My admission to a U.S. university gave me the opportunity to further examine the issue of moral education. I began my investigation by examining the practice of moral education in upstate New York schools. I first visited several Christian schools and then went to some public schools. The moral education practice in the Christian schools was in many ways similar to what I was exposed to in China. Educators in these schools seek to provide a well-rounded education for their students just as Chinese educators do, and they both emphasize students' moral development. Like the Chinese schools, these Christian schools also take a direct and comprehensive approach to moral education. Moral instruction is both a separate curricular entity and an integral part of the regular curriculum. The core of moral education is, of course, the teaching of morals and values. And in this, the uniqueness of Christian schools becomes identifiable. Compared to the Chinese schools, there is nothing unusual about the moral instruction in Christian schools from a pedagogical point of view, but philosophically and ideologically, the difference is significant. The morals and values taught are decidedly based upon the Christian faith. As one teacher in a Christian school claimed, "The ultimate manual/textbook for moral education in our school is the Bible." Values such as love, meekness, respect, fairness, and caring are greatly stressed and are taught as values that were practiced by Jesus Christ and expected of all devout Christians.

In much the same way that Chinese moral education is closely and explicitly tied to larger ideologies, such as communism and Confucianism, Christian schools are not at all apologetic about the ideological underpinning of moral education they engage in. The Christian religion is the fundamental basis and source of that instruction. This very fact caused me to be cautious. Understanding the fine line between public schooling and private schooling in the United States, I rejected any impulse to accept Christian school moral education as the example for public schools.

However, I was impressed by what I observed in those Christian schools. Christian educators' deep commitment for students' moral development was notable as was their holistic/comprehensive approach. I remained wary of the overall religious tone of their definition, explanation, and justification of morals and values; nevertheless, the Christian schools may still offer us some lessons.

My subsequent visits to the public schools reinforced my positive experience with the Christian schools. As my investigation unfolded, I found obvious differences in moral education efforts between the public schools and the Christian schools and, of course, between the public schools and Chinese schools. Moral instruction as a recurrent component of the curriculum is almost nonexistent in the public schools. They approach moral education in a much more informal way than the Christian and Chinese schools do. Lacking any formal programs in moral education, these schools influenced children's morality and character mainly through individual teachers' efforts found in the form of a hidden curriculum. In addition to teacher examples, extracurricular activities, school culture, peer influence, the selection of textbooks, and the instruction process also served as parts of this hidden curriculum. Schools do not have any policies regarding teachers' morally relevant teaching, and teachers may not be aware of what kind of moral philosophy is guiding their instruction. Therefore, moral education is very likely to be idiosyncratic, fragmented, and even inappropriate. No matter how strong a hidden curriculum of moral education might be, moral education in these schools seems to be quite nondirective in nature or, as the Christian educators call it, "a form of moral relativism." I understood the historical and cultural roots of such a practice, but I continually wondered if a more directive approach could have a place in a pluralistic society. Such questioning finally led me to examine character education.

When I first heard of the theory of character education, the most popular approach to moral education in today's United States, I was very excited. I could not resist its temptation since it matched my established notions of moral education so well. I was first attracted to it by its criticism of moral relativism and the nondirective nature of moral education practiced in many American schools. According to Lickona (1999):

> Character education is the deliberate effort to cultivate virtue. Virtues are objectively good human qualities, such as a commitment to truth, wisdom, honesty, compassion, courage, diligence, perseverance, and self-control. Virtues are good for the individual...[and] good for the human community....To be effective, character education must be comprehensive, intentionally making use of every phase of school life as an opportunity to develop good character. (p. 23)

Initially, such claims might seem appealing to many people who are seriously concerned about building children's character and the schools' moral mission. There are indeed some strong points in Lickona's definition. For example, responding to the nondirective nature of moral education in American public schools, Lickona argues that a systemic approach to moral education is necessary, and moral education must become an integral part of the public school curriculum. Schools have both the right and responsibility to engage deliberately, not haphazardly, in moral education efforts. Children's moral development and character building is too important to only be addressed by an informal approach or within a hidden curriculum.

Furthermore, good values indeed are the characteristic features of human well-being and a good society. However, good values do not grow automatically in human life; rather, they need to be cultivated through a positive environment and effective education. In addition, as Lickona argues, education for values and character must be comprehensive, and it should include both direct and indirect teaching. All of these perceived strengths of character education seem to mirror what I learned from the Christian schools, but character educators seem to go well beyond the serious limitations of Christian educators imposed by their religious definition and justification of morals and values. (Of course, Christian educators and others who agree with them could view this as a strength. I'm now speaking from a public educator's perspective.) Character educators claim to teach common or universal values instead of values stemming from or justified by certain religions. Are the "objectively good human qualities" not what we should seek in a culturally/religiously diverse society? In short, upon encountering the theory of character education, I was drawn to its merits.

It is obvious that my initial agreement with Lickona's claims about character education was a reflection of what I had learned in the Chinese educational system and in the larger Chinese culture. For example, there is a clear sign of the well-advocated Chinese idea of a "well-rounded education," and there is an acceptance of the Confucian ethic that human nature is basically good and can be cultivated and improved. Also, I found the direct teaching in moral education legitimate as that had always been how moral education was taught in China.

But gradually, I became skeptical about American character education, especially when I found more and more of a resemblance to Chinese moral education. First, I found a similar rationale. Like Chinese educators, American character educators also pay much attention to social problems and suggest that schools have the responsibility to solve these problems (Lickona, 1993; Ryan 1989). Like their Chinese counterparts, Americans also tend to moralize social, cultural, and psychological phenomena and overemphasize the role of moral education. For example, a starting point of character education advocates is their belief in youth deviance as exemplified by gun violence, teenage pregnancy, and drug abuse. They characterize these social problems as individual problems that reflect a deterioration of individual morality and, therefore, advocate character education as a solution (Bennett, 1992, 1993, 1994; Lickona, 1991, 1993; Kilpatrick, 1992).

This way of thinking is similar to that of Chinese moral educators and raises many questions. It stresses the individual's moral responsibility but ignores the larger social and cultural conditions that construct and define that individual's behavior. Both Chinese moral educators and American character educators emphasize the socialization and enculturation of children by passing on social and cultural norms and inculcating external moral rules while downplaying freedom of choice and the importance of human liberation and social change.

A closer examination helped me see that, like Chinese moral educators, American character educators embrace the "bag of virtues" approach to moral education. Character education is overwhelmingly virtue centered (Leming, 1997; McClellen, 1999; Noddings, 2002). Character educators define character as the possession and manifestation of virtues, and character education as the cultivation of these virtues. Virtues are defined noncontextually as objective and absolute existences (Lickona, 1991, 1999).

Moreover, virtue-centered character education seems to be deeply rooted in certain cultural traditions and carries particular ideological influences. For example, like Chinese educators who openly embrace Confucian ethics, some leaders of American character education explicitly argue for the teaching of traditional American values based on the Judeo-Christian tradition (Bennett, 1993; Wynne, 1989a, 1989b). According to a critic of modern character education, David Purpel (1997), the religious tenor of character education bears an uncanny resemblance to the rhetoric of contemporary neoconservative movements in the political and cultural arenas.

Politicized moral education in China has always been carried out in the name of the people. Similarly, American character educators place strong emphasis upon community. While challenging the individualism that permeates American society, character educators try to restore a spirit of community. However, in emphasizing community consensus on the development of moral values to be taught, they risk sacrificing the interests and values of individuals and, particularly, minorities. Character educators ignore the issues of gender, race, class, and culture in their decision-making process. They overlook the fact that in a community certain subgroups always control the decision-making. While emphasizing community-based decision-making, character educators are likely to be advocating and reinforcing ideologies and values of dominant social groups. In China, moral education is ideologically dictated by the Communist Party and contributes to communist control. We have reason to worry that the emphasis on community consensus in American character education may help create a highly moralistic but not necessarily moral schooling. A moralistic schooling is likely to reinforce the dominant social interests and power relations.

Some leaders of U.S. character education, like Lickona (1999), advocate a so-called comprehensive approach to character education. Questions have been raised, though, about the nature of this comprehensive approach and its relationship to the direct teaching of values. Both critics of character education, such as Alfie Kohn (1997a, 1997b), and advocates, such as Eric Schaps, Esther F. Schaeffer, and Sanford N. McDonnell (2001), have argued that character education programs are dominated by traditional methods of behavioral training. The concern is that the choice of didacticism and indoctrination in character education may make room for conservative ideological representations and fundamental religious impulses. To what extent and in what ways does the character education movement reflect ideological conceptions of schooling and morality? How is morality itself conceptualized?

How are social problems viewed? And how is character education organized? These questions need to be critically examined.

In short, the theory of and rationale for character education, the philosophy and the assumptions underlying it, and its practice and implementation raise political and ideological concerns. Although it has a different face than it does in China, the politics and ideology of character education in the United States represent a reality that needs to be deconstructed.

Making the Hidden Curriculum Explicit and Challenging the Politics of Character Education

The proponents of character education ignore an important fact: Powerful conservative moral training already infiltrates American schools even if it is often in the form of a hidden curriculum. For example, Anyon (1980) explores the actual curriculum of docility and obedience taught to children of the lower classes, while Giroux (1988) describes the hidden curriculum that imposes dominant class values, attitudes, and norms on all students. As will be discussed in later chapters, today's advocates of character education often reinforce this type of conformist moral teaching and strive to transform it to a more directive and systemic approach. It is indeed difficult to find an emphasis in the character education literature on developing thoughtful critics of society's problems and on educating students to engage in social improvement. Why is that? What is it about the nature of the movement that sidesteps such important issues and approaches? What are the origins of character educators' conceptions?

Unlike in China, where the politics and ideology of moral education are quite explicit, the same issues in the United States tend to be more implicit. The increasing popularity of the current character education movement seems to blind educators to the possible dangers of certain political orientations embedded within the movement. Character educators claim support from the American public. As another leader of character education, Kevin Ryan (1989), notes, the public's views of the issue were "registered in the 1975 and 1980 Gallup polls, wherein 79 percent of the respondents indicated they favor 'instruction in schools that would deal with morals and moral behavior' (Gallup 1975, 1980). So, concern there is" (p. 4). However, the polls indicate that people only support a general moral/character education, not any specific character education agenda. As Singer (2000) points out, people

Ideology, Politics, and Moral Education

may "agree with generalities, the 'character education themes,' not specifics—the substance of character education proposals" (p. 275). Everyone may agree that people should have good character, but there is no consensus about what good character means and how it is achieved. The fact is that few are against character education for children because few people are well informed about the political nature of the character education movement.

The debate over character education surfaced in the 2000 American presidential election. When responding to questions and concerns about guns and pornography in American society, Democratic candidate Al Gore and Republican candidate George W. Bush held different opinions. While Gore emphasized efforts for stricter laws on gun control and wanted more restrictions on the entertainment industry, Bush argued that schools must teach character education. Bush (2000) said:

> Gun laws are important, no question about it, but so is loving children and character education classes and faith-based programs being a part of after-school programs...and so there's a—this is a society that's got to do a better job of teaching children right from wrong.

This seems to support what Purpel (1999) argues: "The discussion of character education has come to the point where it has become an overtly partisan political issue" (p. 83). Many agree with Purpel. For example, Singer (2000) believes character education is on the agenda of the Republican Party and religious conservatives. Nucci (1989) also notes that the issue of character education is mostly raised by political and cultural conservatives: "Led by public figures such as former Secretary of Education William Bennett, the political right has called for a return to the direct teaching of traditional values through what is called 'character education'" (p. xiii).

Clearly, character education is preferred by certain political groups and represents specific ideologies, but it is also true that the issue may blur party lines and cross power boundaries. As many advocates of the movement claim, character education has received support from political leaders both on the left and on the right (see Ryan, 1989, for example). Indeed, former president Clinton supported character education in at least two State of the Union addresses. Although the difference in the endorsement of character education between Democrats and Republicans can be seen (for example, the Democrats mostly use the term character education in a general way, without referring to specific religious implications), there indeed exists the possibility that two or more political parties may work together to endorse one conservative ideology represented by the character education initiative.

The party lines do not necessarily divide between commonly held ideologies. As Nelson, Palonsky, and Carlson (2000) argue: "Ideologically, conservatives and liberals share basic beliefs" (p. 308). For example, neither the conservative nor the liberal sees the contemporary form of democracy as problematic, deserving of critical examination. Instead, they both assume the legitimacy of the existing social order and demand that schools maintain the status quo. So, it is not surprising at all if character education, which stresses more conformity and less critical thinking, may find bipartisan or cross-party support.

Any ethical system is always situated within certain social and political discourses. Similarly, any moral education program is also politically charged. There is no politically neutral moral education in the world. Educators must be aware of the political and ideological orientations of moral education efforts in the school and of the politicization they might reinforce through moral education programs they are teaching. Educators must ask and answer questions such as: Who makes the decision about curriculum and instruction in character education? Whose values are taught in the process? Whose interests are met through the program? At present, these questions seem to be either not addressed or addressed superficially. For example, character educators claim to teach "universal values" or "community-based character traits." Difficult, yet legitimate, these questions remain. It is time to openly examine the political nature of character education. Educators have a responsibility to make explicit the hidden curriculum of politics and ideologies in moral education and challenge the status quo of the established moral education practice.

Notes

1. My translation.
2. My translation.
3. My brief review of Chinese moral education may overgeneralize an extremely complex field that has always had many variations in theory and practice. Even within an extremely centralized system, "deviant" practice may occur at local levels. Especially in recent years (starting in the late 1980s), many efforts have been made to break through the centralized curriculum administration. Very often, these efforts have been encouraged, even organized, by the central government. Such efforts include the "One Syllabus,

Many Textbooks" reform, the curricular emphasis on the personal development of the student, curriculum integration in elementary schools, and the school-based curriculum planning. These reform movements have contributed significantly to the change in moral education in schools. While acknowledging these reform efforts, it must be noted that the overall political control in school moral education remains unchallenged. For example, moral education as a separate subject required for compulsory education (grades 1–9) is still obliged to carry out the socialist and communist ideals. The top-down "official knowledge" sets directions even for the school-based curriculum, which is still rarely found nationwide. The politics of moral education continues to be explicit in Chinese schools.

4. My translation.

CHAPTER TWO

The Early Character Education Movement: A Historical Perspective

The cross-cultural journey brings me back to the United States. This chapter explores the battles over morality and character in American schools throughout the twentieth century and focuses on the character education movement in the early decades of that century. This chapter is not meant as a comprehensive history of the moral education movement; I would like simply to develop a historical perspective for a political and ideological analysis of the current character education movement.

Character education is not a modern invention. The term was widely used to describe an educational movement in the early twentieth century. It bears new meanings in our time; yet current practice may be better understood from a historical perspective. As the historian of education William J. Reese (1999) states: "History has a tremendous role to play in explaining the fate of teaching of moral, ethical, and religious values in the schools" (in McClellan, 1999, p. vii).

However, before setting out on the historical tour, we need to develop a framework for the term. In what sense is "character education" used? More specifically, what is the relationship between "character education" and other terms such as "moral education"? It is difficult to define character education because educators disagree over the emphasis and scope of it. The boundary between the two terms, character education and moral education, is also often blurred.

Alfie Kohn (1997a) points out that there are two distinct meanings of the term "character education":

> In the broad sense, it [character education] refers to almost anything that schools might try to provide outside of academics, particularly when the purpose is to help children grow into good people. In the narrow sense, the term denotes a particular style of moral training, one that reflects particular values as well as particular assumptions about the nature of children and about how people learn. (p. 154)

Character education in the broad sense, as Kohn describes it, may be viewed as synonymous with moral education, which can be defined as "a form of education that concentrates on producing moral people" (Noddings, 1992, p. xiii). This study does not define character education in this broad sense; rather, it uses it in the narrow sense of moral training. I consider character education to be a special approach with its own philosophical and pedagogical assumptions among the broadly based school efforts to influence the morality, values, and character of youth. Even if character education, past and present, has been diverse and multifaceted in both theory and practice, its core is still unique and identifiable. For example, both McClellan (1999) and Noddings (1995, 2002) define the typical feature of character education as the inculcation of virtues.

I adopt James S. Leming's (1997) tripartite time line of the development of moral education in the United States:

> Three significant periods of interest in moral education mark the twentieth century—the character education movement of the 1920s and 1930s, the values and moral education movement of the 1970s and 1980s, and, finally, the character education movement of the 1990s. (p. 12)

Character Education in the Nineteenth and Early Twentieth Centuries

During most of the nineteenth century, moral education was a central task of American schools. The Common School movement made public schools the most important educational institutions. By making education universal, Americans hoped to spread a common culture. Moral education was seen as a means to achieve such a goal. According to Michael B. Katz (1971), the moral basis of the movement was a mechanism of social control. Its chief legacy was the principle that "education was something the better part of the community did to the others to make them orderly, moral, and tractable" (p. ix).

The centrality of moral education remained an article of faith from the creation of the public school system. The champion of the Common School movement, Horace Mann, argued that "the germs of morality must be planted in the moral nature of children at an early period of their life" (in McClellan, 1999, p. 18). In addition, "Moral education, or the formation of right attitudes, was more important than learning any skill or subject. Schools existed to serve society by tending to the characters of otherwise neglected children" (Katz, 1971, pp. 31–32).

Moral education was integrated into the entire school life in the nineteenth-century U.S. public schools, especially elementary schools. For example, moral lessons were diffused through textbooks—readers, spellers, and even arithmetic books. Famous spellers and readers, like those of Noah Webster and William Holmes McGuffey, showed a tremendous moral emphasis. The values taught were a blend of traditional Protestant morality and nineteenth-century conceptions of good citizenship. Many values such as diligence, orderliness, docility, punctuality, and willingness to comply with the regulations of an establishment were also consistent with the demands of the increasingly industrial society. As Katz (1971) put it, "The common school made company men" (p. 33). Educators believed in absolute rules in moral training and left little room for interpretation and flexibility.

Social Changes and School Responses

Significant changes began in the last years of the nineteenth century as the school struggled to redefine its functions in response to the demands of a distinctively modern society. The latter part of the nineteenth century was a time of turbulence in American society. The fast-paced technological advances, increasing urbanization, industrialization, and immigration dramatically transformed society and people's lives. The social changes continued in the early twentieth century.

The schools responded to changes in society by changing their attitudes toward and practices of moral education. Educators began to give far more attention to academic and social competence and less attention to religion-based moral teaching. The increasing industrialization, specialization, and the application of science and technology in the production system demanded more solid intellectual training. As a result, religion-based moral training gradually died out in the increasingly secular schools. In 1895, a two-hundred-page report on educational affairs submitted to the National Education Association (NEA) devoted only sixteen lines to moral education (McKown, 1935, p. 75). Traditional moral education in the school had declined greatly.

At the same time, however, many people deplored this decline and began to develop new approaches to moral education in schools. In a necessary response to the new social order, the reformers all attempted to go beyond the nineteenth-century moral training framework but ended up with different schemes of moral education. According to McClellan (1999), two general opposing views on moral education emerged among public educators. The character education effort sought to preserve traditional values in the secular schools. "Usually rallying around one of several programs of 'character education,' those who favored this approach attempted to retain a central place in the school for the teaching of specific virtues and the cultivation of the traits of good character" (McClellan, 1999, p. 48).

The other view of moral education was the product of the progressive education movement. Progressives were deeply skeptical of both traditional moral education and the new efforts at character education. They envisioned a radically new approach to moral education that was more flexible and critical (the progressive view of moral education will be examined in depth later in this chapter). They believed that their approach would meet the evolving needs of an ever-changing society. Despite their novelty, progressive voices did not receive a significant hearing until the mid-1920s. The victor in the battle during the early twentieth century was the character education approach that involved explicit moral training. Character education dominated the discourse of moral education and made a substantial impact on actual school practice.

Advocates of the character education approach analyzed social trends and their impact on the society before introducing their ideas on character building. Their understanding of the social changes provided them with a starting point for their education efforts. Harry C. McKown was an outspoken advocate for character education in the early twentieth century and a prolific writer on the subject. His *Character Education,* published in 1935, was one of the few comprehensive accounts of the movement for that period. The book captured the content and nature of character education programs during the first decades of the twentieth century (Leming, 1993, 1997). McKown's arguments about the connections between social changes and the need for character education are revealing.

McKown described the changes in family, industrial, political, commercial, educational, and religious life. He worried about break-ups in the home, rampant individualism in the workplace, political corruption, negative and biased values in the media, crime, shifting cultural values, and the decline of religion.

According to McKown (1935), the change in the family was "striking and revolutionary" (p. 15). Family members were increasingly employed in

The Early Character Education Movement

widely varying and apparently unrelated occupations. Various educational, social, and recreational institutions and organizations competed with home life to induce people out of the traditional family bond. As a result, the home was losing its power as a multipurpose life center:

> The average home is usually only more or less of a house in which to sleep, and...occasionally to eat....The day of the old red tablecloth has just about gone and the old-fashioned evenings at the fireside have all but disappeared. (p.16)

Outside of the family, former small-scale production units were replaced by larger, complex, and highly specialized factories, companies, and corporations. Specialization reinforced the tide of individualism, but it demanded interdependence and cooperation among workers as well.

Politics was characterized as corrupt. "Probably some of it is green, some ripe, and certainly much of it is rotten" (McKown, 1935, p. 25). Political forces also controlled the media. As McKown (1935) argued, "This most important single educator of the public [the newspaper] frequently has a biased, and often a distorted, but always a powerful, influence on the ideas, ideals, and actions of the members of society" (p. 32).

The increase in crime was tremendous, according to McKown (1935), who estimated a 1,200 percent increase over the past forty-five years [1890–1935]. Meanwhile, there was a remarkable change in people's life styles and after-work leisure activities. He listed a series of newly emerging things during that time, such as the prevalence of dancing, card-playing, and smoking, especially among women; revealing clothing and bathing suits; near-equality of the sexes; frankness in discussing many problems and topics that were formerly taboo; and women coming out of the home to work. With all of these changes in work and leisure, the church became less attractive to people, especially youngsters. McKown noted that the church could not hold a large percentage of the young people any longer. Formal religion was definitely losing its influence.

All of these social changes had implications for education. It was a time for reform. For McKown and other character educators, it was a time to resume moral training and character building in the school.

Character Education for a Better Society and a Whole Person

Character educators had a clear vision of the goals of their efforts. To sum up his observations of the social changes, McKown (1935) stated, "Each and every one of these trends has important moral and ethical implications" (p. 41). He emphasized the need for a virtue-centered moral education to address social problems. Although he realized that the causes of youthful crime were many and varied, and he indeed placed a large share of the blame for crime on society, he argued for a program of educational prevention. He even quoted the ancient Chinese philosopher Confucius to support his idea of virtue-centered character education for crime prevention:

> Guide the people by law, even guide them by punishment; they will shun crime, but will lack shame. Guide them by virtue, even guide them by *li* (mores) or equity and they will develop a moral sense and become good. (pp. 40–41)

Another advocate for character education seemed more direct than McKown when he termed the social problems moral bankruptcy and proclaimed his proposal for character education. James Terry White (1909), whose book was adopted by the influential Congress-chartered Character Development League, wrote:

> The welfare and safety of the State are entirely dependent upon character. Every thinking person knows that one of the greatest needs of the country to-day is a correction of the deplorable laxity in morals. There is danger of moral bankruptcy. More than law and legislation the crying demand is for greater *private* virtue and *individual* integrity. (p. iii)

He used emotional and exaggerated language, such as "entirely," "greatest," "danger," and "crying," to emphasize his points. It is sharply evident that White blamed individuals for the problems found in the society and argued that the problems resulted from individual moral decay. Since private morals and virtues were so crucial for a better State, a virtue-centered character education was therefore urgently needed. As we will see in the next chapter, modern character education advocates, such as Bennett and Lickona, provide very similar arguments for reintroducing character education in schools.

Thus, the new call for moral education was commonly and popularly justified by the so-called moral decline in society. According to the proponents of character education, the moral decline "manifested itself in an increase in the number of divorces, dependent children, suicides, murders, robberies, sales of intoxicating beverages, tobacco, coffee and candy, as well as a disgust with the methods of Standard Oil and the insurance companies" (Yulish, 1980, p. 19). It is noteworthy that public resentment of the domination of certain large corporations was considered a sign of "moral decline." It is also surprising that "eating candy, smoking, and drinking coffee were not viewed as physically harmful, but were seen to indicate a growing desire for mere stimulation of the nervous system and thus morally wrong" (Yulish, 1980, p. 20). The old Puritan values of purity, thrift, and self-control reemerged in the "new" moral education schema.

For these moral advocates, because moral decline was everywhere, moral training through public education was a necessity to shape American society into a purer and nobler national character. Reflecting upon this widespread rationale for moral training in public schools, the NEA sought to become an influential organization in the growth of character education and declared:

> The Association regrets the revival in some quarters of the idea that the common school is a place for teaching nothing but reading, spelling, writing and ciphering; and takes this occasion to declare that the ultimate object of popular education is to teach the children how to live righteously, healthily, and happily....The building of character is the real aim of schools and the ultimate reason for the expenditure of millions for their maintenance. (in Yulish, 1980, p. 28)

It was clearly evident to the NEA that intellectual and academic training should not be the singular, or even the main, aim of public schools. The building of moral character must be the central task of schooling and must be restored to classrooms. This view was clearly in opposition to the idea that schools should emphasize intellectual and academic training, a stance that emerged with growing industrialization and the development of science and technology.

Thus, the call for character education was integrated into a strong concern for the education of the whole child. The proponents of character education pointed to a danger in the one-sided efficiency of modern society. This is a new challenge to youngsters, they maintained, and schools therefore must create a program of moral education to prepare them to become well-rounded persons and operate effectively under the altered circumstances. F. Neff Stroup (1931), superintendent of schools in Newark, New York, summarized the idea of a well-rounded education:

> Character training has come to take on a new meaning. We used to look upon character as the moral development of the child and considered the home and the church largely responsible for this instruction. Now we recognize it as the sum total of

qualities or features which distinguish one person from another. This involves not only the moral or spiritual growth of the child but the intellectual, physical and social as well. (p. 571)

This understanding of character directly led to the ideas for a comprehensive character education program in practice. As we shall see later, most character education programs developed in the 1920s and 1930s were broad in scope—but still narrow at their core. They were concerned with preparing the child for his entire future life in the society. This included lessons in right living, citizenship training, life adjustment, vocational efficiency, and worthy use of leisure time.

With all of these concerns for a better society and the whole child, the school reassumed its responsibility for moral training. As we saw earlier, the former centers of community life, namely, the church and the family, had lost their power in the increasingly impersonal nature of a technological society. Accordingly, their religion-based moral training was seriously jeopardized. With the rising new faith in science, morality became secularized. The State in general and the school in particular were seen as the new bearers of morality. The need for a new form of moral education emerged. As Yulish (1980) puts it, "In order to generate a common ethical base, a perfect civilization, a just society, a kingdom of God on Earth, it was necessary to naturalize the old dream of salvation into the new dream of character formation" (p. 34). The public school was expected to take this responsibility and become the center for moral education.

The call for moral training was also greatly reinforced by the First World War. The war not only reinforced the need for character education, it also provided a particular emphasis. The nationalistic, jingoistic fervor in America during the war pushed the schools to place a stronger emphasis on patriotism, duty, and civic training. Morality largely became civic responsibility. The concept of the good man was redefined to become synonymous with that of the good citizen. This shift greatly influenced the philosophy and implementation of the character education programs in schools.

Character Education Programs in Schools
In this section, the specific efforts of character educators in schools are examined. The section deconstructs the character education program by looking into its objectives, use of character traits, and methods.

The Early Character Education Movement

Objectives. Let us first explore the perceived aims or objectives of character education during that period. Whether or not these aims or objectives were actually accomplished, they served as directives. McKown (1935) listed five objectives of character education, which he claimed to be "fundamental, fairly well agreed upon, bases of character education" (p. 47).

The first objective is "to develop an intelligent respect for the conventions of society" (p. 48). McKown argued: "The individual comes into, and becomes a part of, a very definitely established society, and it is trite to remark that he must learn to conform to the standards of conduct on which this society is based" (p. 48). This argument clearly reveals the author's view of the relationship between society and education: The society is "definitely established" and education has to prepare people to adapt themselves to it. Character education, accordingly, must be a means of socializing individuals, and educators must teach young people to regulate their conduct in the interest of society. McKown emphasized the traditions, attitudes, ideals, and habits found in any given group or community and maintained that they should govern all of the individual's activities. He fully realized and accepted the legitimacy of traditional American schooling when he claimed, "An important function of education in any society, from the most primitive to the most modern, is to teach the child to appreciate and utilize properly the contributions of his ancestors" (p. 48).

It must be noted that McKown was arguing for "intelligent respect" for the conventions of society. He discredited both the complete rejection and the blind acceptance of the traditions and practices of a former generation, but without a doubt, he emphasized respect for society. Failing to address any negative aspects of society, he stressed the conformity of individuals to the "well-established society" and its conventions and rules.

The second objective for character education is "to develop an increasing ability to discern causes and to relate effects" (McKown, 1935, p. 53). It seems that McKown paralleled the process of developing moral character with the process of developing the ability to think rationally. In this sense, character education was expected to prepare individuals to function effectively in different and, especially, in difficult life situations. Character education was designed to teach individuals how to make intelligent choices.

The third objective reads: "To develop a recognition and acceptance of one's responsible membership in society and an increasing success and satisfaction in discharging that membership effectively" (McKown, 1935, p. 56). Again, this objective emphasizes the social life of an individual. McKown stressed the individual's responsibility for "social usefulness" (p. 56) and "larger loyalties" (p. 56) for serving others. Service was an important value and goal advocated by character educators.

The fourth objective reads: "The harmonious development, adjustment, and integration of one's personality" (McKown, 1935, p. 58). This objective emphasizes the individual's harmonious development, both personally and socially. Character education was designed to help integrate all elements of one's personality. Motive, interest, belief, will, and effort should be harmoniously coordinated. Social adjustment and personal adjustment are inseparable, as personal adjustment is necessary for the general good of the society. Character education was "to teach individuals those ideals and habits that will result in the creation of the greatest amount of wholesome enjoyment for the greatest number of individuals over the longest period of time" (p. 59). Thus, morality should not be seen as restricting the pleasure of life. Moral education should make life more pleasant.

The final objective is "to develop the desirable traits of character" (McKown, 1935, p. 63). This objective seems to make a direct connection with the character education programs in the schools. McKown claimed that the general elements of a good character were positive traits or virtues, therefore, the end of character education should be the development of these traits or virtues. According to McKown, the previous four objectives could be integrated into this category. Each objective actually emphasizes one virtue. For instance, the first objective emphasizes respect; the second, reasoning ability (making acceptable choices); the third, service; and the fourth, personal adjustment. McKown (1935) thought that this objective was widely pursued in practice:

> Nearly all of the devices for character education—courses, books, codes, creeds, oaths, pledges, slogans, rating schemes, etc.—stress the importance of the development and correlation of these more or less specific elements, usually illustrating and applying them to as many different situations as possible in the hope that the child will generalize this teaching and apply it to other more or less similar situations. (p. 65)

Many researchers of the character education movement in the 1920s and 1930s examined the "trait approach" to character education and found it to be a major feature of the movement (Leming, 1997; McClellan, 1999; Yulish, 1980). McClellan (1999), for example, argues that it was the use of character traits or conduct codes that clearly set character education off from other moral education initiatives. He notes: "These codes were essentially lists of virtues, sometimes presented in the form of laws or pledges and designed to provide a focus for moral education both in and outside the classroom" (p. 50). As we shall see in later chapters, the definition of character education as the teaching of character traits or virtues is also common to modern character education programs.

Use of Character Traits. We now look into several typical character traits and morality codes of the character education programs. One of the first character education programs was developed in Toledo, Ohio, in 1901. It consisted of a five-minute talk each morning on such traits as obedience, kindness, and honesty. One topic was scheduled for each month (McKown, 1935, p. 76). This was probably the earliest form of the one-virtue-per-month approach, which is extremely popular nowadays.

In 1909, the Character Development League of New York City initiated a plan of using the biographies of great men for character education in public schools and homes. James Terry White's 1909 book was especially written for this purpose. White considered biography "one of the best text-books for character teaching" (p. i). Biography is an example; it brings out the beauty of character and makes righteousness contagious. Learning from biography was believed to allow children to have intimate acquaintance with those who have lived beautiful lives and who have achieved the highest ethical ideals.

In White's book, the series of "character lessons" subdivides good character into thirty-one traits, including obedience, honesty, perseverance, purity, self-control, and patriotism.[1] The author suggested that several traits be taught in each grade. As a whole, the "character lessons" were to be taught systematically throughout each year of the school course. Pupils were not only to understand these lessons but to practice the virtues. All subject teachers were required to combine moral lessons with their class instruction.

The use of character traits was highly regarded by character educators, and there were many competitions to encourage the use of character traits. In 1916, the Character Education Association, a private organization created in 1911, sponsored such a competition. The first-prize winning code, the Hutchins Code, ended up being the most famous morality code of the period. Written by William Hutchins and published in 1917, the Children's Morality Code outlined "ten laws of right living": self-control, good health, kindness, sportsmanship, self-reliance, duty, reliability, truth, good workmanship, and teamwork. These laws provided codes of behavior for physical and mental hygiene as well as morality.

Many schools across the country quickly adopted similar character traits and/or morality codes as a focus for their programs in character education. The traits and codes were directly taught in the programs. McKown (1935) summarized the "direct method":

> The direct method is so named because of its attempt to instill the various virtues by centering attention very directly upon them through discussing and illustrating them; memorizing and reciting creeds, verses, slogans, pledges, golden texts, etc., that suggest them; analyzing men, actions, and events to discover them; writing essays and stories emphasizing them; and applying them directly to the lives of the pupils. (p. 76)

As I will show in later chapters, the focus on a set of virtues, including the means of incorporating them into the academic content of the curriculum and extracurricular activities, is also a hallmark of contemporary character education programs.

Methods. Character educators attempted to integrate character traits or morality codes into all aspects of school life. The codes provided themes for both formal instruction and extracurricular activities.

In 1934, the research division of NEA surveyed character education programs across the country. The NEA survey found that some schools created separate class periods for character education, but most relied largely upon regular classwork and extracurricular activities to stimulate character growth (Yulish, 1980, p. 151). Individual guidance was widely used to enable the pupil to adjust in accordance with desirable standards. The role of teachers was crucial: Teachers were not merely people who imparted knowledge; they were character builders, social workers, counselors, and psychologists.

Group activities played a vital role in the character education efforts. They were important opportunities for students to practice the virtues illuminated in the codes. Clubs, assemblies, athletic programs, student governments, and homerooms were specifically designed for the purpose of character education. Student government was extremely popular during that period. By the mid-1920s, when character education peaked with the extensive use of morality codes, group activities designed for character building were virtually universal. Ninety percent of the junior and senior high schools throughout the country had some form of student government (McKown, 1935, p. 89).

General Trends and Underlying Ideologies
The special features of character education with its objectives, utilization of character traits, and methodology reveal several major trends that characterized the entire movement in the early twentieth century. By examining these trends, we may gain a clearer view of its ideological and political nature.

Being Comprehensive. First of all, character education was designed to be comprehensive, both in its content (aims or goals) and its methods. As was mentioned earlier, character education was a result of the concern with educating the whole child. With moral development as its core, character was recognized as the sum total of qualities or features that distinguish one person from another.

This comprehensive understanding of character was consistent with and integrated into the larger educational reform movement during the period. The major themes of the reform movement included social efficiency, citizenship, and life adjustment. This reform movement produced a document, popularly called "The Cardinal Principles Report," that was "a major landmark in secondary education in the United States" (Kliebard, 1995, p. 96). The most noteworthy portion of the report was the statement of the seven aims to guide the curriculum: (1) health, (2) command of fundamental processes, (3) worthy home membership, (4) vocation, (5) citizenship, (6) worthy use of leisure, and (7) ethical character (The Commission on the Reorganization of Secondary Education, 1918, pp. 11–15).

The report made a close connection between education and the nonacademic activities of people's lives. It called for a curriculum that would produce a well-rounded and actual life. The general acceptance of the recommendations of the report indicated that it overshadowed the humanist approach by the previous Committee of Ten report that advocated traditional academic training. It also marked the comeback of an emphasis on citizenship, character, and other nonacademic aspects of education. The reorganization of the traditional school subjects in terms of the seven aims outlined in the Cardinal report emphasized the need for a comprehensive character education plan.

As we shall see, character education attempted to deal with everything beyond academics that was relevant to the child's development. Therefore, citizenship training, life adjustment, vocational education, and worthy use of leisure time all became the concerns of character education. The concepts of right living, the right work, and the right use of leisure epitomized the moralistic zeal of character education. It was the duty of schools to dictate the right way to live, to act, and to relax.

Yulish (1980) reviewed a number of comprehensive programs in character education during the early twentieth century. Some of his data are used here in the analysis of general trends.

One of the first comprehensive programs in character education was developed by Edwin Starbuck at the State University of Iowa in 1921. Starbuck articulated the notion of the ideal child and the goal of character education:

> A person with powers proportionally developed, with mental discrimination, aesthetic appreciation and moral determination; one aware of his social relationships and happily active in the discharge of all obligations; one capable of a leisure-loving nature, revering human beings, their aspirations and achievements; one observant of fact, respect of law and order, devoted to truth and justice; one who, while loyal to the best traditions of his people, dreams and works toward better things; and one in whom is the allure of the ideal and whose life will not be faithless thereto. (in Yulish, 1980, pp. 107–108)

The allure of that ideal strengthened the author's concern about the preparation of children for life adjustment in the areas of health, group living, civic relations, industrial and economic relations, parenthood, and traditional values. Similarly, in Los Angeles schools, the objectives of character education were stated as vocational efficiency, worthy family membership, good citizenship, and worthy use of leisure time (Yulish, 1980, p. 131).

The emphasis on adjustment and psychological guidance was also clearly evident in a 1929 Utah Plan. The plan not only aimed to promote citizenship training, it was also concerned with alleviating the problems of "maladjusted" children. These children included the mentally retarded, physically defective, emotionally unadjusted, morally handicapped, truants, and daydreamers (Yulish, 1980, p. 114). Thus, character education seemingly became a matter of adjustment. All those who had trouble adjusting to school and society for whatever reason needed character education.

The comprehensive nature of character education was also indicated in the efforts to cultivate all aspects of a child's character: cognition, emotion, and action. For example, a 1927 Nebraska Plan answered the question of how one gets pupils to do what they ought to do, by the following instructions: "(1) Control their feelings; (2) direct their instincts and emotions; (3) persuade their intelligence; (4) influence their habits through (a) conditioning of instincts; (b) forming of sentiments; and (c) modifying their motor adjustment" (in Yulish, 1980, p. 115).

As we have seen, these comprehensive character education programs reflect the principles of the "Cardinal Report," which stresses the broad and varied goals of schooling. However, the core of the comprehensive character education program is still a narrow approach to moral training affected by traditionalist notions of morality and moral education. Moreover, the comprehensive character education programs with a thin core of moral training stress socialization and political control of individuals.

Connecting to Tradition. Another important characteristic of the movement was its close connection to tradition. Responding to a rapidly developing modern society and fearing the so-called moral decline in that society, character educators attempted to retain a central place in the school for teaching traditional values and the formation of good character. They created a new moral education program to prepare people to operate under the altered circumstances. The new program, however, was centered on traditional values, which were believed to be compatible with modern society.

The various character traits and morality codes used in character education programs indicated that their substance was derived primarily from the nineteenth-century morality. For example, similar values could be easily found in the McGuffey readers. Even the fundamental philosophy of character educators was the same as that of their predecessors. As McClellan (1999) revealed:

> These reformers [character educators] saw moral education as fundamentally a problem of motivation, not of ethical reasoning, and they sought to use every means available to them to ingrain good habits and to strengthen the will of students against the temptations of the day. To them, character was less a matter of making fine ethical distinctions than of having the resolve to do the right thing. (p. 54)

To be fair, character educators at that time indeed deserved being called reformers. They understood that the world had changed and were willing to make some compromises with the new twentieth-century life. For example, few of the character education programs gave the morality codes a religious sanction. The approach to character education in the school was apparently secular. Moreover, they paid more attention than their predecessors to the freedom of the learner. For instance, some programs used open-ended techniques, such as debates, and many student groups tried to adopt some mock-democratic procedures (McKown, 1935). Nevertheless, character educators in the early twentieth century still largely continued to do what was done in the previous century and embraced tradition as the major underpinning of the movement. In its basic nature, the character traits endorsed still reflected a Puritan tradition, even though it was implicit.

Emphasizing Civic Values. We cannot overlook the character education movement's emphasis on civic values. Character education reflected a particular type of citizenship education. The church and the family had previously held unrivaled power in the sanctioning of morality and ethical behavior, but the rapid secularization of a growing urban, industrial, and scientific society seriously undermined their authority. The schools thus assumed the responsibility for individual moral conduct and the teaching of moral values.

Educators created a character education program that advocated a State-sanctioned moral system which relied heavily upon the values of loyalty, patriotism, obedience to authority and law, as well as subordination of personal life to the social order. As we saw earlier, character education programs listed "life adjustment" as one of their goals. The precepts of right living were consistent with the values of the dominant elites in the culture and became the criteria of such adjustment. Moral values, if they were useful for the maintenance of the social order, were fostered even though they might be in conflict with an individual's religion or conscience. Obedience to the laws of society made people moral and good.

The goal of an ideal society was ever-present in the minds of character educators and set the boundaries for their educational standards. As the Utah Plan stated, "For a reflective and progressive moral personality, there is an ideal society over and above the actual society and it is this that sets the standards for moral advancement" (in Yulish, 1980, pp. 114–115). In 1926, the Committee of Character Education of the NEA released a report on character education in schools. In terms of the character traits, the committee suggested, "In school life as a whole, the traits of loyalty, responsibility, conformity, cooperation and courtesy were most desirable" (in Yulish, 1980, p. 120). It is evident that the social/civic values took precedence over values such as personal initiative and independence.

The Early Character Education Movement

The emphasis on civic values was obvious in most comprehensive character education plans. The Nebraska legislature enacted a Character Education Law in 1927 to provide the legal authority for the State Department of Public Instruction to develop programs in character building. According to Bill 79-2131, it was the duty of each and every teacher in the first twelve grades of any public, private, parochial, or denominational school in the State of Nebraska to give special emphasis to

> common honesty, morality, courtesy, obedience to law, respect for the national flag, the Constitution of the United States and of the State of Nebraska, respect for parents and the home, the dignity and necessity of honest labor and other lessons of a steadying influence which tend to promote and develop an upright citizenry. (in Yulish, 1980, p. 123)

Worthy character was thus seen as the basis of good citizenship, and the school was the State's means of training its citizens. People were considered primarily as citizens. Their conduct and behavior were to be shaped and controlled in order to produce good citizens. As the distinctions between morality and citizenship became blurred, character education turned into the means of political control.

A Social Movement. This section looks at the leadership of the character education movement and how it reflected certain social interests and forces. The strongest leadership of the movement came from outside the circle of education. As McClellan (1999) points out:

> From the beginning the movement had its greatest successes at the local level rather than in the great national forums of educational discourse, winning impressive support from state legislature, state and city schools boards, private benefactors, and a variety of newspapers and popular magazines. (p. 49)

During the fervor for the use of the morality codes, a then-popular magazine, *Colliers Magazine,* distributed a third of a million copies of its codes to the nation's schools (McClellan, 1999, p. 51). This is just one example of how the character education movement had become a social movement, one which had crossed the education boundaries and broached broader social interests.

We have discussed the various character education programs in the states. State legislatures and boards of education played a key role in the initiatives.

Politicians' roles in advocating character education were influential. In 1934, Royal S. Copeland, Chairman of the Senate Subcommittee on Racketeering and Crime, led a campaign to strengthen schools in their battle against antisocial tendencies in children. Senator Copeland insisted that teachers be more responsible for the social and moral adjustment of their pupils than for their intellectual development. As a result of his pressure, the Seventy-Third Congress added $70,000 to its ten-million-dollar budget for the study of character education in Washington, D.C. The character education experiment in Washington, D.C., was mainly designed to fight the antisocial tendencies in children that supposedly led to juvenile delinquency and crime. Many of Senator Copeland's addresses in support of a nationwide program of character education and citizenship training for the prevention of crime appeared in the *Congressional Record* (Yulish, pp.138–142).

Many organizations outside of the education community, according to McKown (1935), had been actively involved in the efforts of character education and served as partners of the schools. Among these organizations were the Boys Scouts of America, the Junior Red Cross, the Girl Reserves (part of the Young Women's Christian Association), the 4-H Clubs (part of the service program of the United States Department of Agriculture and the State Colleges of Agriculture), and the Sportsmanship Brotherhood. These organizations, with their own distinctly conservative political agendas, worked with the schools on character education.

As we shall see, these major trends in the early twentieth century all re-emerged in the modern character education movement, albeit in different forms. This central point is important: They not only remind us of the historical continuity of character education but also help us understand the sociopolitical nature of the current movement.

Criticism of Character Education and Its Decline

Character education was pervasive in American schools in the first three decades of the twentieth century, but its influence began to decline in the late 1920s. McClellan (1999) summarizes the causes of this decline:

> The decline was partly a product of a growing impatience with conventional moral restraints, an impatience reflected in a variety of colorful ways in the 1920s. It was also partly the result of a concerted attack by progressive educators, who pressed their case with increasing urgency in the 1930s when economic and social dislocations seemed to call for a more critical approach to moral education. (p. 55)

The Early Character Education Movement

Progressives considered character education a continuation of the traditional moral education, which they felt should be abandoned in order to make moral progress in the new social order. They embraced science and reason rather than religious or other authoritative doctrines for solving complex moral and social problems. Their attack on character education directly targeted the use of morality codes and the teaching of particular virtues. They did not believe that memorizing morality codes would help make moral people. They argued that virtue-centered character education could not affect the long-term behavior of children.

Progressive educators saw an emphasis on particular virtues not only as useless but also harmful to ethical living in modern society. Simple codes of conduct were unable to guide people in the ever-changing modern world. As John Dewey (1909) argued, "We need to see that moral principles are not arbitrary, that they are not 'transcendental'; that the term 'moral' does not designate a special region or portion of life" (p. 58).

Under the highly specialized and segmented modern situations, progressives urged that obedience to authority and conformity to tradition, as represented by the character education approach, must be thrown away. They argued for ethical flexibility and relativity. As the progressive version of the 1932 report of the Character Education Committee of NEA's Department of Superintendence clearly declared:

> Relativity must replace absolutism in the realm of morals as well as in the spheres of physics and biology. This of course does not involve the denial of the principle of continuity in human affairs. Nor does it mean that each generation must repudiate the system of values of its predecessors. It does mean, however, that no such system is permanent; that it will have to change and grow in response to experience. (in McClellan, 1999, p. 56)

Because ethical behavior is related to particular situations, moral or character education must ensure that the child's moral character will develop in a natural and social atmosphere (Dewey, 1934). By the progressive definition of moral education, schools must teach constructive reactions to life's extraordinarily varied contingencies. Progressives advocated a moral education that did not teach specific moral precepts or encourage particular character traits but rather cultivated in students open-mindedness and a general ability to make moral judgments. This model of moral education encouraged a spirit of inquiry and imagination and stressed reasoning and problem solving.

Progressives also criticized character educators' attention to matters of private conduct, such as drinking habits and sexual conduct, and paid far more attention to larger social and political issues. For progressives, character had more to do with the ability to contribute to the creation of a more humane and democratic society. As Dewey (1909) wrote:

> The moral has been conceived in too goody-goody a way. Ultimate moral motives and forces are nothing more or less than social intelligence—the power of observing and comprehending social situations—and social power—trained capacities of control—at work in the service of social interest and aims. (p. 43)

It was argued earlier that character education blurred the distinction between character education and citizenship education and emphasized the obedience of individuals to the State and the well-established society. Progressive views of moral education, however, stressed individuals' roles in the change of society.

One research study that focused on the character education movement gave a fatal blow to it and put the champions of character education into a defensive position. The study was the now-famous Hartshorne and May Study (1928–1930) by Hugh Hartshorne and Mark May. Conducted when character education was in its heyday, the study represented the most systematic inquiry of that movement and the best research on it in that period.

The purpose of the study was to determine the effects of moral education, both secular and religious, on students' character-related behavior. The researchers adopted multiple research methods and activities for their inquiry (Hartshorne & May, 1975, pp. 8–9). The student sample for the actual survey was large with over 10,000 school children participating in the study for the first volume of its report (Chapman, 1969, pp. 58–59).

The report of the study was published in three volumes, *Studies in the Nature of Character: Volume 1, Studies in Deceit* (first published in 1928); *Volume 2, Studies in Service and Self-control* (1929); *and Volume 3, Studies in the Organization of Character* (1930). These volumes found, astonishingly, that character education programs had no significant positive effect on the conduct of students. The study raised serious questions about the effectiveness of didactic instruction in the popular character education programs and on relevant important philosophical and psychological issues. For example, at the close of the first volume, Hartshorne and May (1928/1975) discredited the "objectiveness" of the moral ideal and argued for the situatedness of virtues:

> An individual's honesty or dishonesty consists of a series of acts and attitudes to which these descriptive terms apply. The consistency with which he is honest or dishonest is a function of the situations he is placed so far as (1) these situations have common elements, (2) he has learned to be honest or dishonest in them, and (3) he has become aware of their honest or dishonest implications or consequences. (p. 380)

They went on to draw implications for moral education:

> The mere urging of honest behavior by teachers or the discussion of standards and ideals of honesty, no matter how much such general ideas may be "emotionalized," has no necessary relation to the control of conduct....The prevailing ways of inculcating ideals probably do little good and may do some harm....The large place occupied by the "situation" in the suggestion and control of conduct...points to the need of a careful educational analysis of all such situations....The association of deceit with sundry handicaps in social background, home condition, companions, personal limitations, and so on, indicates the need for *understanding* particular examples of dishonest practice before undertaking to "judge" the blameworthiness of the individual....The main attention of educators should be placed not so much on devices for teaching honesty or any other "trait" as on the reconstruction of school practices in such a way as to provide not occasional but consistent and regular opportunities for the successful use by both teachers and pupils of such forms of conduct as make for the common good. (pp. 413–414)

Similar findings and conclusions were provided in volumes 2 and 3. The influence of the Hartshorne and May Study was widespread and significant. It provided strong research evidence on the ineffectiveness of virtue-centered character education programs. Many later theorists and educators draw from the conclusions of this study to critique traditional character education approaches.

Although character education continued to exist in American schools, it was never a star on the stage again until the 1980s. People who had maintained their support for the traditional character education approach had to wait painfully for half a century while reluctantly witnessing the appearance of other approaches to moral education. The new approaches essentially represented a continuation of criticism the progressives initiated in the 1920s.

Moral Education in the 1960s and 1970s:
Continuous Critiques of Traditional Character Education

Formal moral education, characterized by the virtue-centered character education approach, began to decline in the late 1920s and early 1930s. However, the decline of moral education in the next two decades was not dramatic. Actually, both the Second World War and the early stages of the Cold War seemed to emphasize the importance of character. Schools, accordingly, kept offering activities to promote moral and civic growth in students. Schools were expected to play an important role, via moral education, in promoting the values of democracy and battling against the forces of authoritarianism. Under such circumstances, the sharp differences between virtue-centered approaches and progressive efforts toward moral education also seemed to have been replaced by an eclectic and accommodating spirit (McClellan, 1999).

Despite the support for character education from many organizations and the dedicated work of many educators to maintain traditional character education, the overall place of moral education in the school continued to erode in the 1940s and 1950s. The shift in educational priorities marked the time. The call for more academic skills and less moral training once again surfaced and soon won the debate.

McClellan (1999) summarizes three developments that seemed to play a significant role in the erosion of moral education in the school in the 1940s and 1950s. First, a growing need for high-level technical and scientific skills, as associated with revolutions in science and technology, pushed schools to place greater emphasis on intellectual achievement and basic academic skills. More resources were moved to college preparation; "soft" courses and activities in character education were trimmed. Second, the pervasive anticommunism reduced other moral energies of the society and lessened the focus on character education. Teaching national loyalty and cognitive skills that would contribute to the economic and military competition with the Soviets seemed to exhaust the schools' responsibilities for character and citizenship building. Finally, a tendency to draw a distinction between private and public realms and to establish different behavioral norms was growing. Schools, accordingly, began to avoid discussion of morals. Americans of the postwar era increasingly thought of religion and morals as personal and private and assigned the responsibility for them to home and church (McClellan, 1999, pp. 73–75).

With all of these working forces against moral education, by the 1960s, deliberate moral education as represented by the traditional character education approach was in a full-scale retreat in the nation's schools. Throughout the 1960s and 1970s, schools either rapidly adopted an attitude of careful neutrality regarding moral questions or became entirely indifferent to them. A number of social and cultural upheavals helped make moral education problematic for the public schools. As McClellan (1999) argues, "The effort to end racial discrimination, the waging of an unpopular war, a deepening cultural pluralism, and a growing willingness to expand the range of acceptable personal conduct all worked to weaken the commitment of schools to moral education" (p. 75).

In an era full of social tensions, people lost their faith in the existence of a common ground. Cultural relativism became a primary social value. A civil libertarian critique of schools was also rising. Schools were criticized as authoritarian institutions that smothered creativity and enforced a dull conformity. Schools' role in socialization, especially in the realm of moral and political values, must be limited. The radical social critique moved in the same direction as public opinion. A large number of Americans came to distrust established institutions including schools, to fear imposition, and to treat values as purely private matters. Hence, schools tried to avoid controversial moral questions and elevated tolerance into the primary value. Educators backed away from anything that might be labeled "indoctrination." The atmosphere that supported moral education as a primary goal of the school was lost. By the end of the 1970s, the traditional, content-based moral education had reached a historic low point in the nation's public schools (McClellan, 1999, pp. 75–78).

The mid-1960s started a slow revival of interest in new forms of moral education. Several dramatically new approaches gradually emerged and entered schools. Among them, values clarification and the cognitive developmental approach became the most influential. Influenced by and largely remaining within the progressive tradition, these two approaches opposed the traditional virtue-centered character education in many respects. Embracing the spirit of the day, the proponents of these new approaches found character education at best incomplete and at worst threatening to individual freedom and social/cultural diversity.

Values Clarification and the Cognitive-Developmental Approach to Moral Education

According to Louis E. Raths, Merrill Harmin, and Sydney B. Simon (1966, 1978), the authors of the theory of values clarification, values constitute the central part of a moral and civil life. They claim that a value is simply any psychological factor that tends to direct some of the behaviors of a person. Any set of values a person holds does not have to be accepted according to a particular moral standard. However, values should be internally consistent. Hence, the objective of moral education in a democracy is to help students develop internally consistent sets of values and live deliberately by whatever sets of values they individually develop.

Like the progressives, advocates for values clarification consider the process of moral decision-making situational. They deny the meaning of learning any fixed values but emphasize personal and individual values. Unlike character educators who socialize and inculcate students according to presumed moral norms of society and culture, values clarificationists help students choose and develop their own values. Teachers are not the authority figures they were in character education. They should be non-indoctrinating and nonjudgmental to help students discover, choose, and refine their values. It is unjustifiable for a teacher to impose her or any others' values on students; this act of oppression would undermine the individuality and autonomy of students. Role modeling and exhortation of values stressed by character educators are not emphasized in values clarification. Instead, teachers encourage dialogue and discussion among students.

The cognitive developmentalists, led by Lawrence Kohlberg, differ from values clarification advocates in that they accept the existence of absolute values such as justice, the perceived central value. They maintain that people at different levels of moral development differ in their underlying conceptions of justice and their solutions to ethical problems, but their view of values is different from that of traditional character educators who emphasize values as rules for behavior. In direct opposition to character education, moral education for developmentalists means education for moral development, but the process of moral development is not a straightforward acquisition of established norms of the society. According to Kohlberg (1975):

> An adequate morality is principled, that is, that it makes judgments in terms of universal principles applicable to all people. Principles are to be distinguished from rules. Conventional morality is grounded on rules, primarily "thou shalt nots" such

as are represented by the Ten Commandments. Rules are prescriptions of kinds of actions; principles are, rather, universal guides to making a moral decision. (p. 50)

Cognitive developmentalists believe that moral action is mainly a function of moral judgment and that moral reasoning underlies moral judgment. "Moral judgment," Kohlberg (1975) declares, "while only one factor in moral behavior, is the single most important or influential factor yet discovered in moral behavior" (p. 50). By stimulating higher levels of moral reasoning, the school may not guarantee better behavior, but it can make a significant contribution toward that end. Therefore, the purpose of moral education is to improve students' ability and skills in moral reasoning and help them attain the highest level of moral development. Educators using this approach dismiss the "bag of virtues" approach, the teaching of a specific set of values, but emphasize moral reasoning through reflection, perspective taking, conflict resolution, and autonomous choice.

Values clarification and the cognitive-developmental approach enjoyed popularity for about three decades until the 1980s, but criticisms accompanied them from the very beginning. According to critics of values clarification, the content is controversial and the process relativistic. They argue that the proponents of values clarification consider values as ultimately personal and that the implicit message is that there are no right or wrong values. Thus, they maintain that values clarification offends community standards and undermines accepted values. Values clarification does not induce a search for consensus; neither does it stress truth and right behavior nor distinguish morality as a generalizable system of norms from a morality as a system based on personal preference or whim. It purports to clarify values which may not yet exist; what is worse, it fails to discriminate between sound values and a child's egoistic desires (Benninga, 1997).

Although the cognitive-developmental approach has not been charged with moral relativism, it could not escape criticism either. According to Chazan (1985), the focus on justice is unwarranted because many other values cannot be reduced to justice. The method of moral education that focuses on reasoning is rather narrow. Moreover, its emphasis on rights and fairness reflects a masculine bias. In other words, while emphasizing moral reasoning, a cognitive process, it slights the affective components of morality. For example, Carol Gilligan (1982) examined women's moral development and found that women speak "in a different voice" than men. Caring and interpersonal responsibility constitute women's presumably unique moral vision.

Nel Noddings (1984) further addressed a "feminine approach," namely, caring, as an alternative approach to ethics and moral education.

According to critics Devine and Wilson (2000), the cognitive-developmental approach is based on cognitive developmentalism and uses highly unusual dilemmas in moral reasoning.[2] It can become an intellectual parlor game and might have little to contribute to real moral development. It can lead to sophistry, that is, to skill in argumentation in defending even obviously immoral positions. The critics argue that before one can benefit from reasoning about a moral dilemma, one must have a good character in order to evaluate what is at stake. Therefore, they definitely welcome a different approach to moral education.

The different approach they embrace is a new version of character education. Actually, the most severe criticism of values clarification and the cognitive-developmental approach come from the steadfast proponents of traditional character education, such as William Bennett (Bennett and Delattre, 1978). In a climate that favored a return to tradition, the United States witnessed a resurgence of character education in the 1980s.

Notes

1. The complete list of "traits of character" (in the author's order) includes: obedience, honesty, truthfulness, unselfishness, sympathy, consecration to duty, usefulness, industry, perseverance, patience, self-respect, purity, self-control, self-reliance, fortitude, courage, heroism, contentment, ambition, temperance, courtesy, comradeship, amiability, kindness to animals, justice, habits, fidelity, determination, imagination, hopefulness, and patriotism.
2. Discussion of dilemmas was the most important method Kohlberg and his followers used to measure children's moral judgment and moral reasoning, especially during Kohlberg's early research career. The standard dilemmas are context free, hypothetical, and primarily ethical dilemmas dealing with justice issues. The best-known dilemma is the Heinz dilemma. In the story, Heinz's wife was dying of a terminal disease. He heard that a druggist had a new drug which could save his wife. However, the drug was so expensive that Heinz couldn't afford it. So, he pleaded for the druggist to sell the drug at a cheaper price or allow him to pay for it later, but the druggist declined. Without any other solutions available, Heinz must decide whether he should steal the drug to save his dying wife. In the discussion, researchers asked children such questions as "Should Heinz steal the drug or not?" "Was the druggist right that he declined Heinz's plea?" "If Heinz stole the drug, should he be found guilty in the court?" Besides the standard dilemmas, researchers also designed practical school dilemmas to evaluate moral reasoning by pre-

senting real-life situations in a familiar context. See Power, Higgins, and Kohlberg (1989) for more examples of dilemmas.

CHAPTER THREE

Moral Decline and the Politicization of Character Education

The resurgence of character education began in the early 1980s. Since then, character education programs have been implemented in schools throughout the country. Meanwhile, national and local organizations have been created to advocate for the movement; university-based centers and institutes have been established to theorize the initiative; and conferences, workshops, and training programs have been set up to prepare the practitioners. Support for character education at the end of the twentieth century and the beginning of the twenty-first century seems stronger than at any time since the 1950s. As McClellan (1999) comments:

> Disturbed by both the erosion of moral education and by what they perceived to be dangers in values clarification and cognitive-developmental schemes, these groups [proponents of character education] mounted the strongest campaign for virtue-centered education the nation has witnessed since the early twentieth century. (p. 89)

It is significant that character educators often justify the movement by pointing to a moral decline in society. They assert that the moral decay is severe and has largely resulted because schools are not doing a good job with the moral education of youth. Blame is also placed on parents and the media. In order to build a better society and produce moral people, character educators argue for the return of traditional virtue-centered character education to schools.

The claim of moral decline has been with us since the days of Socrates. As chapter 2 outlines, moral deterioration was a strong rationale for the new character education programs in the early twentieth century. Today, similar claims of the "decline and fall of American civilization" and "troubling trends in youth character" (Lickona, 1991, 1993, 1996) serve as a powerful impetus, pushing the movement forward. Such claims have significantly influenced teachers' conceptions of youth problems and education. For example, in 1999, after the shocking Columbine High School shooting in Littleton, Colorado, Thomas Lickona's The Center for the 4th and 5th Rs at the State University of New York College at Cortland sponsored a summer institute on character education. At the conference, I witnessed teachers' great enthusiasm for character education as the solution to the problem of violence. Although those teachers had justifiable concerns about violence and understandably highlighted the role of personal morality and school programs in addressing the problem, they largely downplayed the social and cultural context of youth violence and failed to take into account the economic, political, and cultural practices that have created the problem.

This chapter explores the politics and ideologies embedded in the claim of moral decline and the call for character education. I first introduce the social background of the 1980s school reform movement, of which character education was a part. Then I examine how character educators define social problems such as violence and drug abuse as moral decline and posit character education as the solution. I also explore the social and cultural roots of youth problems, including the immediate environment of child development and the larger sociocultural context. I finally discuss how character educators scapegoat youth and reinforce the socialization of youth to the established social order.

School Reform in the 1980s:
The Fight for Common Culture and Return to Tradition

The claim of moral decline and the call for character education was heard during the larger social and educational reform movements that started in the 1980s, a problem-filled stage of capitalist development in the United States. Character education was officially introduced during a transition period of American capitalism at the dawn of the twentieth century as an individualistic competitive structure became the contemporary corporate form. The transition created social dislocation, breakdown of the traditional family and community units, and other changes in people's lives. The evidently critical relationship between education and the economy emerged, and the use of education as a tool of social policy was emphasized (Bowles & Gintis, 1976). Corporate leaders, politicians, and many educators advocated schooling as the solution for the all-too-evident social ills. Character education, especially, was stressed as the panacea to restore law and order in society.

History seemed to repeat itself more than half a century later. American capitalism had worked well for the two decades following World War II. However, starting in the 1960s, America's dominance of international economic, political, and military matters was challenged. As Shea, Kahane, and Sola (1989) analyze, the U.S. economic "stagflation" largely resulted from an emerging global economy and, particularly, a new international division of labor. The United States had lost its competitive advantage in labor-intensive industries. The capital flight to Third World countries and high-tech mechanization of the workplace had a dramatic impact on the workforce. In addition, the United States was facing strong competition from other capitalist economies such as Japan and West Germany. Economic and social lives were greatly affected by the new technologies and demographics. The increasing use of computers, electronics, robotics, and a vast array of telecommunication equipment had a major impact on corporate production and operation systems. Higher levels of skill were demanded of workers. However, rapidly changing demographics challenged such a demand. Students of the 1980s came from vastly different family structures, economic conditions, and cultural backgrounds.

A portrait of America revealed a bleak landscape: America was more illiterate, more hungry, more homeless, more unemployed, more alienated, and more hopeless than ever before in the nation's history. It was strongly argued that there was a mismatch between the personnel demands of an emerging high-tech, high-skill economy and an increasingly ill-prepared personnel supply from largely poor, minority, single-parent households. Thus, the schools actually became the focus of the debate, but unfortunately the focus was on assigning blame:

> American workers are making substandard contributions to economic productivity. Schools are indicted for undermining the nation's industrial, commercial, technological, and military supremacy and in the world economy by turning out students who have antiquated personality habits and deficient academic skills. In order to restore military supremacy and economic predominance in the international economy, a more direct link is called for between a reformed educational system and a more productive economy. (Shea, Kahane, & Sola, 1989, p. 12)

There was a bipartisan campaign to link the United States' deteriorating economy overseas with the so-called failures of public education (Pinar, 1994). Echoing the business leaders' argument that part of the problem was a lack of motivation in the modern corporate workplace, mainstream politicians and many educators began to seriously address the issue of character again. Character education was thus reintroduced into American schools and expected to carry out the critical task of maintaining the capitalistic spirit.

In the rest of this section, the analysis focuses on one active and influential figure on both political and educational fronts during that period, William Bennett, who became one of the most famous proponents of modern character education. The analysis reveals how the reintroduction of character education was linked to other aspects of the social and educational reform movements of the period and how the underlying rationale for character education was conceptualized.

Bennett published *The De-Valuing of America: The Fight for Our Culture and Our Children* in 1992. That book, one of a series, chronicles his decade of service in the Reagan and Bush administrations as chairman of the National Endowment for the Humanities, Secretary of Education, and director of the Office of National Drug Control Policy. Bennett argues for a particular cultural and educational agenda.

Bennett (1992) believes that the condition of American culture is "troubling." Over the last two decades, he argues, there has been an all-out assault on the common sense and common values of the American people by a liberal elite among academics and intellectuals, in the artistic community, and in the media. He contends that the liberal elite questions the commonly accepted "American dream" and advocates an "adversary culture" that is contradictory to the "common culture" which embraces "the traditional values of the American people." Bennett (1992) bemoans "a cultural breakdown of sorts—in areas like education, family life, crime, and drug use, as well in our attitudes toward sex, individual responsibility, civic duty, and public service" (p. 33).

Without attempting to explore the problems of the existing political and economic systems in the country, Bennett believes that "the issues surrounding the culture and our values are the most important ones" (p. 36). These issues necessitate a systemic cultural reform: a struggle for the "common culture." Educational reform is part of this struggle. The call for "common culture" largely served as the backbone of a systemic education reform agenda.

The criticism of U.S. public schools launched by Bennett and others in the early 1980s was that schools failed to serve the public. Educational standards were low. Students were not learning enough to compete in the world market: American children were lagging far behind their counterparts in other industrialized nations in mathematics, science, and other key academic subjects. The reform agenda, therefore, called for higher standards, the promotion of a national curriculum and national assessment, and a return to traditional schooling (National Commission on Excellence in Education, 1983; see also Ravitch, 1995, for a critique of American education and an advocacy of standards).

This position drew strong criticism. For example, there were those who argued that the so-called crisis in education was "manufactured" and claimed a brighter picture of education and student achievement (see Berliner & Biddle, 1995, for example). Some researchers sifted more carefully through the evidence and took a more balanced approach to the issue (see Stedman, 1995, for example). They found that student achievement in America has historically been low, suggesting a serious long-standing concern that needs addressing, but they also noted that Bennett and others have largely exploited the evidence and exaggerated the decline. Given the historic pattern of poor achievement, the call by Bennett and others for schools to go back to old-fashioned teaching and learning is unjustified.

Nevertheless, character education proponents embrace the darker view of American education and link low academic standards with declining morality. Drawing on many reports of the defects of American public school education, such as the famous 1983 report, *A Nation at Risk*, Bennett targeted the "entire mediocre education enterprise in America" (p. 47). His major reform prescription is a return to the basics and tradition. He consistently talks about "Three Cs"—content, character, and choice. He urges schools to teach a "sound common curriculum" emphasizing traditional academic subjects in liberal arts, moral character, and standards of right and wrong.

Overtly embracing the spirit of the Common School movement in the mid-nineteenth century, Bennett (1992) believes that "improving American education requires not doing new things but doing (and remembering) some good old things" (p. 56). He thus urges today's schools to be committed to the old "faith that public education could teach good moral and civic character from a common ground of American values" (p. 58). He urges an "explicit teaching" of "values that all American citizens share" and regards such teaching as "the legacy of the common school," "a legacy to which we must return" (p. 58). He believes a critical task of schools is "enculturation, the passing on of our values, in an often hostile atmosphere" (p. 35).

The call for traditional common moral education is consistent with the attack on multiculturalism. Standing with other influential writers such as E.

D. Hirsch, Jr. (1987) and Allan Bloom (1987), Bennett (1992) warns of the so-called divisive nature of multiculturalism and calls for a renewed curricular focus on cultural commonalities shaped by Western tradition. Multicultural education, as promoted by Banks (1996), Diaz (2001), and many others, aims to change the curricular and cultural contexts of schools, embrace cultural diversity among students, create equal opportunities for disadvantaged groups, and represent the views of the marginalized or excluded. On the contrary, critics of multiculturalism, like Bennett (1992), defend the standardized presentation of the dominant white, Western, and male-oriented culture in the traditional curriculum. They envision schools as beacons of a single unified high culture, passing on the best that is thought and known in the world. The best, for Bennett and his supporters, is unarguably the traditional canon, the best representation of Western civilization centered on the Holy Scriptures of Judaism and Christianity and other "great books" of Western tradition. Traditional morality and moral education are undoubtedly integral elements of this tradition.

The Claim of Moral Decline and the Call for Character Education

To support their call for traditional moral education, proponents of character education construct a seemingly logical rationale. They systematically describe a serious moral decline in the society, claiming that the overall moral, sociocultural, and behavioral conditions of American society are troubling as indicated by widespread problems such as crime, violence, drug abuse, sexual promiscuity, and other deviant behaviors, especially among young people. They argue that (1) these problems are signs of moral decline; (2) these problems can be seen as moral problems; and (3) these problems are actually caused by the moral decline or moral poverty. Based on these allegations, they conclude that only a virtue-centered moral education could solve these problems.

The Existence of Moral Decline
Character educators use statistics to support their claim that Americans have serious social and moral problems. William Bennett can be seen as an early representative in this regard. In *The Index of Leading Cultural Indicators: Facts and Figures on the State of American Society* (1994), Bennett empha-

sizes the "troubling" condition of American society and provides statistical and numerical breakdowns, charts, graphs, and analyses of the data on crime, family and children, youth pathologies and behavior, education, popular culture, and religion.

According to Bennett (1994), total crimes, violent crimes, and juvenile violent crimes all have increased. Meanwhile, the condition of the family and children has deteriorated while illegitimate births, single-parent families, and divorce rates have increased. His comments on these problems are straightforward (and problematic, I will argue later). For example, he views illegitimacy as "the single most important social problem of our time—more important than crime, drugs, poverty, illiteracy, welfare or homelessness because it drives everything else" (p. 48).

The picture of American youth is dark: Both births to unmarried teenagers and teen pregnancies have increased. For example, he reports, "The rate of births to unmarried teenagers has increased almost 200 percent since 1960" (p. 72) and "The number of unmarried teenagers getting pregnant has nearly doubled in the past two decades" (p. 74). Bennett's portrait of education is particularly pessimistic. According to him, student achievement has decreased as SAT scores have declined and discipline problems have increased. His statistics also show that American children watch too much TV. Sex and violence are pervasive on TV as well as in movies and music. Meanwhile, religion is losing its believers.

Bennett (1994) draws this conclusion: "Over the past three decades we have experienced substantial social regression.... *Unless these exploding social pathologies are reversed, they will lead to the decline and perhaps even to the fall of the American republic*" (p. 8). Obviously, he refers to violent crime, illegitimate births, children living in single-parent homes, divorce, and the drop in SAT scores as "social pathologies," and argues that they "have gotten worse" (p. 8).

Bennett does not overtly claim that all the problems reported are moral problems, but he does emphasize the moral implications of these problems by mixing them together in phrases such as "the moral, social, and behavioral conditions." For him, the social pathologies clearly reflect moral decay. When addressing the lack of moral education in society as the cause of all of these problems, it is clear that he emphasizes the link between these problems and individual morality.

Bennett is not alone in such a critique. Another character education leader, Thomas Lickona, also makes sweeping claims of a moral decline.

Lickona routinely opens his call for character education by claiming that the United States is in "deep moral trouble." For example, in his widely publicized 1991 book, *Educating for Character: How Our Schools Can Teach Respect and Responsibility,* he justifies the case for character education with "accumulating evidence of a moral decline, first in society at large and then among the young" (p. 12). While Bennett focuses on larger "social pathologies" and attention-getting issues such as violent crime and drug abuse, Lickona (1991) sees many phenomena and behaviors, from high-level greed and deceit in politics and business to rule-breaking by ordinary people, as "signs of a moral decline" (p. 12). Although Lickona also draws on statistics to define the problems, more often he uses informal surveys, personal stories, and casual anecdotes to show that moral slippage is everywhere in our society. His signs of moral decline include employee theft, phony resumes, drunkenness, and people who deceive their best friends and cheat on their marriage partners as well as on their tax returns (p. 13).

Moral decline is best shown in youth trends, argues Lickona (1991, 1993, 1996). He repeatedly remarks on "ten troubling trends in youth character" to show that "the general youth trends present a dark picture" (Lickona, 1991, p. 13). These trends include rising youth violence, increasing dishonesty (lying, cheating, and stealing), growing disrespect for authority, peer cruelty, a resurgence of bigotry on school campuses from preschool to higher education, a decline in the work ethic, sexual precocity, a growing self-centeredness and declining civic responsibility, an increase in self-destructive behavior, and ethical illiteracy.

Again, Lickona does not always provide hard data for all of these allegations but very often relies on folklore-type personal accounts to emphasize the broadness and seriousness of the problems and to draw generalizations. For example, in his 1991 book, after describing several cases, such as sixth-grade kids writing sexual notes to one another and teenage girls having babies, he generalizes that there is serious "sexual precocity and abuse" (p. 16) among children and teenagers. Similar generalizations are also given on other so-called indicators of moral decline, including the "increasing self-centeredness and declining civic responsibility" (p. 17) and "self-destructive behavior" (p. 18). Thus, Lickona claims that American society is suffering a serious moral decline.

Moral Decline as the Root Cause of Social Problems

Character education leaders claim that moral poverty has caused social pathologies such as crime and drugs. In Bennett's (1994) opinion, even if we face a serious "social regression," the overall political and economic systems are fine: "The United States has the strongest economy in the world, a healthy entrepreneurial spirit, a still-healthy work ethic, and a generous attitude—good signs all" (p. 8). For him, the capitalist economic production machine runs well; the social resources are fairly distributed; and the political system is just and effective. In a word, the social structure has few and inconsequential problems, but the general picture of the social and cultural conditions of the United States is still dim, and we still suffer severe social pathologies and behavioral problems. Why has this happened and how can we deal with it? As Bennett (1994) answers: "The social regression of the last 30 years is due in large part to the enfeebled state of our social institutions and their failure to carry out a critical time-honored task: the moral education of the young" (p.12). He is clear about one thing: Loss of morality matters most; failure in moral education results in social regression.

In their book, *Body Count: Moral Poverty...and How to Win America's War against Crime and Drugs*, Bennett, Dilulio, and Walters (1996) go further and emphasize "moral poverty" as the root cause of problems such as crime and drugs. They first emphasize the seriousness of crime and drug problems. They argue, "While it is true that the nation's overall crime rate has leveled off in recent years, crime rates today remain far higher than they were when our parents and grandparents were growing up in this country" (p. 19). Their portrait of juvenile crime is just scary:

> America is now home to thickening ranks of juvenile "super-predators"—radically impulsive, brutally remorseless youngsters, including ever more pre-teenage boys, who murder, assault, rape, rob, burglarize, deal deadly drugs, join gun-toting gangs, and create serious communal disorders. (p. 27)

According to their version of what has caused crime and drug abuse, "the nation's drug and crime problem is fueled largely by moral poverty" (p. 14). They have determined that "today's lack of self-restraint and social norms, the breakdown of civil society, the attenuation of individual responsibility and commitments, and the importance of religious faith" are at the root of problems of crime and drugs (pp. 14–15). While stressing moral decay as the cause of these problems, they denigrate all other explanations of the causes of the problems, especially the analyses of "root causes" (economic poverty, racism, and lack of government-funded social programs).

If problems such as drugs and crime have resulted from moral poverty, moral education presumably becomes the solution to the problems. As Bennett (1994) claims, "We desperately need to recover a sense of the fundamental purpose of education, which is to engage in the architecture of souls" (p. 12).

Lickona agrees with Bennett that moral education is the only answer. Lickona (1993) believes that "troubling" youth behavioral trends are convincing evidence that we are largely failing to transmit our most basic moral values to the next generation. Then he blames schools for not doing a good job in moral education. Lickona nostalgically recalls the old days when "schools tackled character education head on"—through discipline, the teacher's example, the daily curriculum, the Bible as sourcebook, McGuffey readers, and lessons about honesty, hard work, thriftiness, patriotism, and courage. Even if he never explicitly calls for bringing the Bible back to today's classrooms, he praises old character education practices which were grounded in religious traditions (I will readdress the religious influences in character education later).

Lickona then rebukes several powerful forces that have caused old-fashioned character education to crumble. He criticizes Darwinism, logical positivism, personalism, pluralism, secularization of the public arena, and individualism for leading people to think of morality as being in flux, relative to the individual, situationally variable, and essentially private. Without giving a comprehensive and dialectical analysis of the impact of these forces on the society, Lickona denounces them as barriers to achieving moral consensus, which he sees as indispensable for character education in the public schools.

Like Bennett and Lickona, other character education leaders frequently addressed similar concerns about the so-called moral decline in society and the failure of moral education in schools (Kilpatrick, 1992; Ryan, 1989; Wynne, 1989a, 1989b). They often draw upon similar statistics to support their arguments. While emphasizing the statistic numbers, they failed to check the validity of the figures in the statistics and failed to examine the real meanings and implications of the data. For example, none of them seriously investigated how morality could be involved in such problems as the drop in SAT scores and rising rates of out-of-wedlock births. No one ever questioned whether the problems indeed represented a moral degeneration.

The campaign for traditional moral education initiated by politicians and educators such as Bennett and Lickona largely set off the entire modern character education movement. Bennett's role in the movement has been pioneering. The Chinese government has a direct and controlling impact on the school curriculum; Bennett, of course, did not have that sort of power. However, his role as Secretary of Education still allowed him to have a significant influence on the movement. As Bennett (1992) himself notes, "What the Secretary of Education can try to do is influence the direction of federal programs, reinvigorate a national discussion about education, highlight what works and what doesn't, and set in motion constructive changes" (p. 68). Bennett's efforts served as an "initial push" for the character education movement (Leming, 1997). As a college professor in teacher education, Thomas Lickona may have had a more direct influence on the practice of character education in schools. He has written many books and articles on the subject and taught courses on character education. His annual summer institutes on character education have drawn a large number of classroom teachers from all over the country.

Moral Decline: Misrepresentation of Evidence

Moral Decline: An Overstatement

Character education advocates' claims about moral decline need to be critically examined. They provide some important information about the conditions of American society and raise some concerns about certain social problems; however, upon closer examination, these claims are problematic. In Bennett's 1994 book, statistics on crime, drugs, family structure, or religion are hardly exclusive indicators of the comprehensiveness and complexity of the society. Statistics on each of the social indicators are limited and do not indicate the depth and breadth of a particular social aspect. For example, his data on education are restricted to the change in SAT scores, several samples of subject-based international assessments, and an informal teachers' survey on discipline problems. He relies on such limited data to conclude that the entire educational system has failed.

More importantly, character educators misinterpret important data and overlook significant competing data when discussing social issues. Many of the phenomena Bennett (1994) discusses (such as the increase in single-parent families, the rise in the divorce rate, and the decrease in church membership) are controversial and are not commonly viewed as signs of social pathology. But Bennett pronounces them serious social ills. The same statistics he provides on crime, drugs, and education may be reinterpreted to suggest different conclusions. For example, *The Statistical Abstracts of the United States* (the major source of Bennett's index) clearly shows that the overall crime rates in the last two decades have steadily decreased. The decrease in the 1990s, when Bennett wrote the book, was even more significant. Bennett ignored the decrease. For each category—total crimes, violent crimes, or juvenile violent crimes—Bennett, by drawing eye-catching charts, finds that the numbers have increased. However, the increase in total numbers does not necessarily mean that the problem is becoming worse when one realizes that the population has increased.

As Bennett (1994) himself acknowledges, overall drug use rates have decreased significantly. He states: "Overall drug use among Americans is down more than 50 percent from its peak in the late 1970s....Among adolescents, drug and alcohol use is at its lowest since monitoring began in 1975" (pp. 38–40). Nevertheless, he still emphasizes the seriousness of the problem by documenting the total number of drug addicts.

Sexual misconduct may not be as serious as character educators claim either. Character education writers, especially Lickona, often assert that there is an epidemic of sexual promiscuity among youth. Lickona often exaggerates atypical and informal data, such as kids writing sexual notes, to support his claim. The validity of his generalization is thus seriously undermined. According to many government agencies such as the Centers for Disease Control and Prevention and the Federal Interagency Forum on Child and Family Statistics and news sources such as *Newsweek* and ABC Broadcasting, both teen pregnancy and teen birth rates have significantly dropped in the past decade. But even though the rates are still high, as character educators may emphasize, it is problematic to claim that teen pregnancy and teen birth reflect sexual promiscuity among teens. The data do not indicate who the putative fathers of these babies are. Many argue that, often, they are older men. Therefore, teen pregnancy is not predominantly a problem of teen girls.

What about the case of violence? The overall youth crime rate is decreasing. According to *America's Children: Key National Indicators of Well-Being, 2002*, developed by the Federal Interagency Forum on Child and Family Statistics, since 1993, both the violent crime victimization and offending rates for youth aged twelve to seventeen have decreased by about 65 percent. Despite the shocking incidents in the news about violence in schools, school safety experts say such incidents are rare. According to the Justice Policy Institute, there is only a 1 in 2 million chance of being killed in a U.S. school. School violence seems more prevalent these days because those rare incidents generated a lot of media attention. Along with other incidents, the Columbine shooting fueled the public perception that our schools are dangerous places. Right after that shooting, according to a Justice Policy Institute report in 2000, seven out of ten Americans said that they believed a shooting was likely to occur in their local schools (Sealey, 2001). Such an opinion is obviously generated by fear, not fact.

As we have seen, character educators' interpretation of statistics is troublesome. They heavily and uncritically draw on official statistics, but even these official statistics may carry certain validity problems. According to sociologists Adler and Adler (2000), "Although official statistics yield information about a broad spectrum of people, they may be fairly shallow and unreliable in nature" (p. 95).

Joel Best (2001), a University of Delaware professor of sociology and criminal justice, examines "bad statistics" and urges us to "approach statistics critically." He examines a statistic ("The number of American children killed each year by guns has doubled since 1950.") from the 1994 report on *The State of America's Children Yearbook* of the Children's Defense Fund, a well-known advocacy group for children. This statement is subject to different interpretations and may represent an outright impossibility. Take any number other than zero in 1950 and start doubling it; in a couple of decades the number of deaths would be astronomical and by now it would be greater than the population of the whole country. Many other questions could also be raised. Where did the statistics come from? Who counts child gunshot deaths and how? What is meant by a "child"? What is meant by "killed by guns" (gunshot death statistics often include suicides and accidents as well as homicides)? Best (2001) points out that people rarely ask such critical questions when they encounter statistics.

Did character education writers, such as Bennett and Lickona, ask critical questions about the very similar statistics on the so-called social pathology or moral decline? They did not. Consider Bennett's treatment of the SAT data in his 1994 book. He reports that "Scholastic Aptitude Test scores among all students have dropped 73 points from 1960 to 1993" (Bennett, 1994, p. 84). He relies on this statistic as an important indicator to draw the conclusion that American education as a whole is in decline.

Bennett's treatment of the data and resulting claim is subject to a serious critique. The SAT is a poor barometer of general school performance. According to Stedman (1993), "The most serious limitation of the SAT data...is their lack of relevance as a measure of school quality" (p. 218). First, the SAT is only taken by certain college-bound students and does not represent the typical student. Second, the SAT is designed to predict this selective group's future college performance and ignores most of the high school curriculum. Such irrelevance is even noted by one of Bennett's political allies, Lynne Cheney, who points out that "looming over our educational landscape is an examination that, in its verbal component, carefully avoids assessing substantive knowledge gained from course work" (in Stedman, 1993, p. 219). In addition, the test is technically flawed. As Stedman points out, the rapid-fire processing of sentence completions and math puzzlers is hardly a good way to judge students' achievement in school.

In addressing the decline in the SAT scores, there is something important that Bennett has overlooked. As Stedman (1993) argues, "The decline largely reflects enormous changes in the population of test-takers that resulted from the expansion of educational opportunity in the 1960s and 1970s" (p. 218). In agreement with Stedman's argument, Rothstein (2001) notes that the SAT and ACT are voluntary tests. The number of students taking the tests has, in fact, increased greatly over the past several decades. By itself, this increase should push average scores down, because more modest achievers are now participating, whereas high achievers have always taken the test. Thus, the decline can largely be traced to the population increase and the increased percentage of students who apply to college. That results remained steady or even declined a little, in spite of changing demographics, may suggest real gains rather than a loss.

Failing to see the whole picture of American education, Bennett exaggerates the decline in achievement. Even if we cannot overlook the deep, long-standing academic and other problems that are embedded within our schools and the need for fundamental school reform, we cannot accept Bennett's claim that our schools are collapsing. Emphasizing the decline in the SAT scores, Bennett minimizes the importance of expanding educational opportunity. As Stedman (1993) points out, taking the SAT used to be a privilege of mostly white, male, and middle-class students bound for Ivy League colleges, but today the SAT is taken by more than a million students (over one quarter of them are minorities), and many of these students have lower socioeconomic status. It is no wonder that the scores have dropped, given these students' weaker preparation and the often inadequate state of minority schooling.

Contrary to Bennett, we can see the change in the SAT scores less as a measure of educational decline and more as a sign of the expansion of equal opportunity, which must be regarded as historical progress. Bennett's overemphasis of the failure of current schools is consistent with his return-to-tradition reform agenda. But as Stedman (1993) warns us, "We should all have serious doubts about a so-called golden age of education and be leery of solutions to today's problems that are justified primarily by wistful references to the past" (p. 216).

Rothstein (2001) correctly points out that many leaders today seem to look for negative news about student performance. Why do they? One explanation might be that politicians do not want to spend more money on education. Education Secretary Rod Paige in 2001 complained that test scores had not improved despite record levels of spending on education over the last decade. This is exactly what the former Education Secretary Bennett claimed about ten years ago. As Bennett (1994) emphasized, "There is no systematic correlation between spending on education and student achievement"(p. 83).

Even if we do not have reason to refute all of the character educators' data and analyses, our reinterpretation of the data and introduction of competing data suggest the validity problems of their claims. Though crime, drug abuse, sexual misconduct, and violence do exist, the claim that they are serious, widespread, and out of control seems exaggerated. Exaggeration of the seriousness of the problems does not help solve them. We need to clearly define the nature and scope of the problems in order to find effective solutions. Spina's (2000) warning of the misconception of school violence is revealing. As she notes, we do not intend to downplay the tragedy of school shootings or to minimize the expectation that schools should be absolutely, not relatively, safe, but we must understand the level of fear and resources surrounding the so-called epidemic of violence in schools.

In addition, even if we admit that there are indeed serious problems in society and among youth in particular, the criticism of youth behavioral problems by character educators is overstated and inappropriate. By such criticism, they produce and spread an abnormal fear of youth deviance. Many people dabble to greater or lesser degrees in various forms of deviance. Studies of juvenile delinquency suggest that participation in some forms of delinquency is extremely widespread, nearly universal. How many people can claim to have reached adulthood without experimenting at least once with drinking, speeding, drug use, or vandalism? Yet, how many of these people are considered deviant or to have serious problems? Not many. Very few people would remain unmoved by the blood-stained school shootings, but not many would interpret such common behaviors as drunkenness or speeding as signs of moral decay. Most of us tend to accept the existence of these behaviors in some form, without saying they are morally right, and do not believe they will cause our republic or civilization to crumble.

According to renowned sociologists Emile Durkheim (2000) and Kai Erikson (2000), deviant behaviors are inevitable in all societies, and in many situations deviance may be viewed as normal rather than pathological, as serving a positive function in society. Deviance reminds us of a society's moral boundaries. As Erikson said:

> Deviant forms of behavior, by making the outer edges of group life, give the inner structure its special character and thus supply the framework within which the people of the group develop an orderly sense of their own cultural identity. (in Adler & Adler, 2000, p. 14)

Because deviance plays a role in defining morality and bringing people together, we should recognize its importance as a social function. We do not have to amplify the already loud cries of moral breakdown and social disintegration from character educators.

Let us examine this further. Statistics are just tools used for particular purposes, and people with different political agendas use statistics to promote all sorts of causes. Bad statistics or misinterpretation of statistics may be used to stir up public outrage or fear, to distort our understanding of the world, and to lead us to make poor policy choices. We have seen the troubling ways character education leaders present statistical data. In Bennett's (1992, 1994) works, he overemphasizes certain data, misinterprets other data, and overlooks competing data. Also, in Lickona's (1991, 1993, 1996) works, he features dramatic and compelling examples to claim moral decay, accepts an example as a typical case, and ignores the possibility of an example serving as an extreme, exceptional instance. The result is that fear has been generated, and a seemingly strong rationale for moral training has been created. We then must ask: What is their purpose? What is their political agenda?

Deviance and moral decline as concepts are man-made constructs. As Adler & Adler (2000) argue, "the social constructionist perspective suggests that deviance should be regarded as lodged in a process of definition, rather than in some objective feature of an object, person, or act" (p. 133). Also, as

Becker (2000) notes, "The deviant is the one to whom that label has successfully been applied; deviant behavior is behavior that people so label" (p. 78). From this perspective, deviance lies in the eye of the beholder. There is nothing inherently deviant in any particular act until powerful groups define the act as deviant. Though such a perspective may imply problematic relativism, it reminds us that deviance and moral decline are socially constructed.

Advocates for character education such as William Bennett represent powerful groups in our society that control the political, economic, and cultural resources. In the process of making the case for moral decline and campaigning for character education, they act as "moral entrepreneurs" (Adler & Adler, 2000) and try to define public morality. They create legal definitions of human conduct, casting as criminal those behaviors that threaten their own interests. They justify and disseminate their ideologies of morality, deviance, and crime. As we have seen, advocates of character education draw on statistics, use dramatic cases, and sometimes borrow research to paint a horrifying picture of youth and youth problems in the public's mind to inspire fear and loathing. While creating a moral panic, they turn to athletes, actors, religious leaders, and media personalities for moral endorsements. For example, the national character education conference invited the "Miss America 2000" to be its keynote speaker. "The rhetoric of the claims tends towards the moral high ground, with attacks on opposing views, while disavowing special interests and asserting the pursuit of the public good" (Adler & Adler, 2000, p. 134).

Moral entrepreneurs crusade to transform certain behaviors into deviant acts. Though inevitably their actions are based on their own moral philosophy and ideology, they claim their position as absolute and essential to protect and preserve the moral code of society. They are self-righteous, but they use strong humanitarian overtones: "The crusader is not only interested in seeing to it that other people do what he thinks is right. He believes that if they do what is right it will be good for them" (Becker, 2000, p. 139). The moral crusader is inclined to be pessimistic about human nature. As we will see in the next chapter, character educators like William Kilpatrick (1992) and Edward Wynne (1989a, 1989b) promote the idea of original sin, dwelling on the difficulties of getting people to abide by the rules and on the characteristics of human nature that lead toward evil behavior.

Because of their pessimistic view of human nature, character educators emphasize moral training and control. Politicians and members of the upper classes such as Bennett and Lickona hold and control the social, political, economic, and moral resources. They have the ability to dominate, both materially and ideologically, the subordinate groups. One way to ensure domination is to pass and enforce norms and rules that maintain one's own position and to define others' behavior as deviant. As we witness the laments for moral decline and the call for moral training, we must not forget the role of power.

Moral Poverty Has Caused Social Problems: An Unfounded Allegation

Having cast a doubtful eye on character educators' claim of serious moral decline, I will now discuss their assertion that moral poverty has caused social problems. In this section, I will examine what has caused such social problems as violence and drug use and argue that the assertions of character educators, especially Bennett, Dilulio, and Walters (1996), are largely unfounded.

Bennett and others attempt to present shocking images of social conditions, particularly those of youth crime, to inflame people so that they respond emotionally and do not examine closely the causes of such crimes. They purposefully and unadvisedly discredit the analyses of "social roots" and deny that poverty is a root cause of crime. Contrary to their denial, many influential sociologists and criminologists of the twentieth century have concluded that poverty and joblessness indeed breed crime. For example, after an extensive review of influential empirical research on the relationship between economic conditions and crime rates over several decades (1950s, 1960s, and 1970s), William Luksetich and Michael White (1982) argue that the empirical research strongly supports the economic theory of criminal behavior:

> There is a significant relationship between economic conditions and the amount of crime. Increases in the unemployment rate are predicted to be associated with increases in the amount of crime....The relationship between income and the amount of crime is predicted to be inverse; that is, the lower an individual's income, the greater is the likelihood of involvement in criminal activity. (p. 144)

Their review particularly focuses on research of economic conditions and youth crime. The conclusions are significant: Deteriorating labor market conditions for youth contribute to the increase in youth crime; there is a strong inverse relationship between low income and arrest rates for juveniles.

Moral Decline and Character Education

Bennett, Dilulio, and Walters (1996) remain skeptical of these findings and arguments. They cite James Wilson, who writes:

> It is far from clear that giving more opportunities or higher incomes to offenders will lead them to commit fewer crimes, and it is even less clear that programs designed to make society as a whole better off will lower the crime rate. (in Bennett, Dilulio, & Walters, p. 41)

Bennett, Dilulio, and Walters (1996) especially remind us that government-funded programs have not eliminated crime and that there is "crime amidst plenty" (p. 41). Government-funded programs may not have eliminated crime because, after all, these programs have not eliminated poverty. The programs have been insufficiently funded and often failed to reach many, sometimes even a majority, of those targeted. Moreover, the programs have largely been welfare-type ones that do not alter the nation's economic structure, a structure which has been the major cause of inequality and poverty.

There has been "crime amidst plenty" because there has always been relative deprivation. Even when fortunes are rising, there always are certain groups in poverty. This was true even in the 1960s about which Bennett, Dilulio, and Walters (1996) commented on extensively. As Bennett, Dilulio, and Walters emphasize, crime rates increased during the 1960s even as the aggregate unemployment rate decreased. But as Phillips, Votey, and Maxwell (1972) inform us about that period:

> Labor market conditions may have improved for adults, but they clearly deteriorated for youths...the generally deteriorating labor market conditions for youths during the 1950s and 1960s was a major contributing cause of the rapid increase in youth crime during this period. (in Luksetich and White, 1982, p. 148, 151)

Bennett, Dilulio, and Walters (1996) argue:

> While objective material circumstances apparently do play a role under some conditions, each of many different types of criminal behavior has many possible "root causes." Economic poverty never stands alone as a determinant of crime, and deviant, delinquent, and criminal behavior never occurs in a social vacuum. (p. 42)

The understanding of the multiple causes of crime is correct, but the failure to recognize poverty as one of the most important root causes is equally serious. Even if they occasionally mention the role of poverty in crime, they tend to remove it from their analysis.

Bennett, Dilulio, and Walters's (1996) treatment of the relationship between crime and racism is also problematic. They emphasize crime as a problem of "sin, not skin" (p. 22). However, many smokescreens surround such a statement. The authors seem to support equality of races by not emphasizing skin color, but they disingenuously claim that all people in this country enjoy the same economic and political rights and opportunities. They seriously overlook the social issues behind skin color, hiding the fact that, in reality, blacks and Latinos suffer systemic inequality because of their skin color. Contrary to Bennett, Dilulio, and Walters's argument, some crime is indeed related to people's skin color. Crime is not caused solely by the so-called "sin" of moral poverty but by racism and other problems from which minority groups in this country have historically suffered.

Bennett, Dilulio, and Walters (1996) deny racism as a cause of crime by stating that "racism is an even less persuasive explanation for the present-day crime problem than poverty" (p. 43). They argue that racism is not the serious problem that it used to be: "Few criminologists would argue that the current gap between black and white levels of imprisonment is mainly due to discrimination in sentencing or in any of the other decision-making processes in the criminal justice system" (p. 43). Given that minorities are more segregated into impoverished and dangerous, crime-ridden communities, they would be more likely to commit crimes and more likely to be jailed. The contention that the criminal justice system is not racist is deceptive. There is ample evidence of serious racism in the U.S. criminal justice system. According to many empirical studies, such as those conducted by Mendez (1983), Kempf and Austin (1986), Sarri (1986), Zatz (1987), Gross and Mauro (1988), and Jackson (1989), for identical or similar crimes, blacks receive longer sentences than whites, and white juries disproportionately sentence blacks to harsher sentences.

Similarly, Fine and Weis's (1998) ethnographic investigation of "cops, crime, and violence" in poor urban neighborhoods reveals a widespread concern that the police force is racist. When asked about violence in their communities, blacks and Latinos focused their comments on "state-initiated violence," detailing incidents of the racist police actions toward men of color, such as harassment and brutality, false arrest, planting of evidence, and exaggerated charges.

After examining the way violence is portrayed in the media, it becomes evident that a strong racial bias has emerged. Cases involving white kids from small towns and suburbs of the American heartland are highly visible, while killers and victims who are poor, predominantly black and Latino, living in inner-city neighborhoods, receive less media attention. If white kids are killed, the incidents become unacceptable to the white-dominated media. When gang violence and deadly shootings occur in poor and minority neighborhoods far away from the lives of white decision-makers, white-dominated communities pay little attention. However, a case of white teens being gunned down in a suburban high school is cause for alarm because the victims could be their own kids. The intense media coverage of the recent school shootings in which the killers and the victims were all white kids from suburban middle-class families seemed to indicate that those shootings were novel in this country.

The point is not that racism directly causes crime (even if it does in some cases). My argument is that racism is usually interrelated with other social factors and plays a role in subordinating blacks and other minorities, placing them at the edge of the society and putting them into at-risk positions. The justice system, police, and media may be complicit in this endeavor. Racism is often entangled with poverty and often puts people of color into disadvantageous positions. As Currie (1993), Hsieh and Pugh (1993), and many other researchers found, jobs and factories have left minority-concentrated urban communities across the United States. The power of unions has declined in the urban Northeast, and the tradition that formerly bonded new generations to stable jobs and life roles has been broken apart. The consequences of this economic community-based bankruptcy are numerous. Among these consequences are the increasing problems of drug use and violence.

Even Bennett, Dilulio, and Walters (1996) themselves acknowledge that race and poverty are connected to crime. They report that residents of Philadelphia, Pennsylvania's largest urban metropolis, experience more murders and other crimes than do citizens of other parts of the state and that young black males are involved in such crimes at a much higher rate than are young whites. According to their book, "42 percent of all violent crimes committed in Pennsylvania occurred in Philadelphia, which contained only 14 percent of the state's population" (p.23). And "in one predominantly black and Latino neighborhood known to residents and police as 'the Badlands' (part of census tract 176 on the map), the murder rate was over 100, more than four times the citywide average of 23" (p. 23). And "almost all of Philadelphia's 89 juvenile victims were nonwhite" (p. 23).

Thus, crime in Philadelphia is closely related to economic conditions and race. This fact may have complex implications. However, Bennett, Dilulio, and Walters (1996) have chosen to avoid touching upon the complexity of the issue. Instead, they lead readers to their simplistic conclusion: Criminals suffer the breakdown of the traditional family and the resulting moral poverty; more specifically, some racial groups suffer more moral poverty. As they claim:

> Black-white differences in rates of criminal offending reflect the fact that, on average, black children are more likely than white children to grow up without two parents or other adults who supervise, nurture, and provide for them...race is, in effect, a proxy for the density of stable, consistent adult supervision in the lives of at-risk children. Give black children, on average, the level of positive adult social support enjoyed by white children, and the rates would reverse themselves. (Bennett, Dilulio, & Walters, 1996, pp. 22–23)

Adult supervision is indeed important for children's growth and may be important for crime prevention. Many black and Latino children may indeed lack such adult supervision and nurturing. Blacks and Latinos are often poorer than whites. In poor minority households, single parents or parents working at two jobs are unable to afford good day care and adequate supervision for their children. Unsupervised kids are, of course, vulnerable to street gangs and crimes. Thus, the contribution of poverty to the high crime rates of these groups must be considered.

If black and Latino children lack adult nurturing and supervision more so than white children, it is probably due to the more serious economic poverty and racism under which their families and neighborhoods have been suffering. The change in family structure is fundamentally a result of social change. All forms of family dysfunctions have deep social and economic roots. Unemployment, loss of jobs, flight of capital to the suburbs, and nonunionized work have produced or contributed to family breakdowns.

Bennett, Dilulio, and Walters (1996) stick to the belief that the fundamental cause of predatory street crime is moral poverty. As they claim:

> In prison or out, the things that super-predators get by their criminal behavior—sex, drugs, money—are their own immediate rewards. *Nothing else matters to them.* So for as long as their youthful energies hold out, they will do what comes "naturally": murder, rape, rob, assault, burglarize, deal drugs, and get high. (p. 28)

Moral Decline and Character Education 77

They further state:

> Many of these super-predators grow up in places that may best be called criminogenic communities—places where the social forces that create predatory criminals are far more numerous and stronger than the social forces that create decent, law-abiding citizens....At core, the problem is that most inner-city children grow up surrounded by teenagers and adults who are themselves deviant, delinquent, or criminal....The problem is not merely that so many inner-city children grow up insufficiently socialized to the norms and values of a civilized, noncriminal way of life, but they grow up almost completely unmoralized and develop character traits that are more likely to lead them into a life of illiteracy, illicit drugs, and violent crimes than into a life of literacy, intact families, and steady jobs. (p. 28)

These claims clearly view children's immediate environment and moral upbringing as the root causes of crime and other problems. No one can deny the environmental factors in shaping crime. The problem is that Bennett, DiIulio, and Walters define the environment exclusively in terms of morality. They argue that children surrounded by immoral and deviant people are themselves likely to become immoral and deviant. However, one must ask what has shaped people's morality or deviance. They never attempt to answer this question. They fail to examine the surrounding issues of morality and only claim that morality is independent of larger social conditions.

In addition, their charge that inner-city children lack morality is offensive and could even be considered racist. They argue that the entire poor minority community—"most inner-city children," not just some in the most difficult conditions—"grow up surrounded by teenagers and adults who are themselves deviant, delinquent, or criminal" (p. 28). They thus condemn the entire inner-city minority population as deviant, delinquent, and criminal. Kids in these communities grow up not just insufficiently socialized but "almost completely unmoralized" (p. 28). In other words, they believe inner-city minority kids suffer a complete lack of morality. Such an assertion is highly disputable and even outrageously false.

Bennett, DiIulio, and Walters (1996) list some typical characteristics of moral poverty such as lack of impulse control and lack of empathy (p. 57). Again, there is some truth in such an argument. In most cases, it is fair to say that criminals might lack a conscience and probably lack a sound moral education, and most killers or drug abusers may lack self-control and empathy. However, any serious analysis must go further. Crime involves values and value choices, but qualities such as self-control and empathy do not develop in a vacuum. Values develop within environmental influences. It is too easy to blame only the criminals for their crimes. We may need to include moral poverty in our analysis, but it is not the fundamental cause. We must find the environmental roots beneath the personal characteristics.

To expound on the issue of individual responsibility in crime, Bennett, Dilulio, and Walters (1996) discuss the relationship between liquor and disorder. They make the connection between drinking and crime by suggesting that alcohol, like drugs, acts as a "multiplier" of crime: "Alcohol figures prominently in disorder and crime—especially in poor, minority, inner-city neighborhoods, where liquor outlets cast their shadows everywhere" (p. 66). This might be true. However, they do not bother to tell us what causes the epidemic of alcohol abuse and crimes, especially among poor people.

Kozol (1992) also writes about problems such as alcohol abuse, gambling, and prostitution prevailing in some inner-city neighborhoods, but comes to a different conclusion. In extremely poor North Lawndale, Chicago, Kozol found that the neighborhood had only one bank and one supermarket but 48 state lottery agents and 99 licensed bars and liquor stores. He argues that economic decline is the root cause of these problems. As he notes:

> Between 1960 and 1970, as the last white families left the neighborhood, North Lawndale lost three quarters of its businesses, one quarter of its jobs. In the next ten years, 80 percent of the remaining jobs in manufacturing were lost. (p. 42)

While businesses were leaving the area, liquor stores were entering. As a result of this trend, criminal activities were sprouting. As Kozol detailed: "As the factories have moved out…the street gangs have moved in….With the arrival of the gangs there is, of course, more violence and death…. Kids…will kill each other over nothing—for a warm-up jacket" (p. 42).

It was largely race-related poverty that caused the epidemic of alcohol consumption, and accordingly, crimes and violence in those neighborhoods. But Bennett and his followers continue to blame the drinkers themselves and label them as morally decadent and see moral poverty as the single root cause of crimes. As noted by Bennett, Dilulio, and Walters (1996), increased alcohol consumption is associated with increased crime, and interventions that reduce drinking may also reduce violent crime and related disorders (p. 66). But we have to remember that, in most cases, in the streets of poor neighborhoods, it is joblessness and the resulting hopelessness that have caused the problems.

However, Bennett, Dilulio, and Walters (1996) believe:

> Social regeneration depends on *individual* [italics added] citizens living better, more committed, more devoted lives...just lives that reflect the basic and modest character traits—*self*-discipline [italics added], civic-mindedness, fidelity to commitments, honesty, responsibility, and perseverance...and to accomplish these things, it would be no small help...to remember God. (p. 207)

The prescription is thus individual self-improvement and personal salvation. Bennett's summary finally comes to an end: "The religious dimension of moral poverty is the most important dimension of all;" accordingly, "the most obvious answer—and perhaps the only reliable answer—is a widespread renewal of religious faith and the strengthening of religious institutions" (p. 208). Given the problems with their analysis and the inherent constitutional problems with religious instruction in public institutions, such a conclusion is unjustified.

We should fully realize that there are indeed crimes in our society and behavioral problems among young people. There are indications that over the past generation or two some crimes have become more egregious, particularly in school settings. However, we must carefully look at the context of the formation and development of these problems. We cannot view violence and drug abuse simply as individual behavioral problems caused by a lack of morality, even though the moral implications cannot be ignored. These problems do not represent solely an individual moral decay; rather, they reflect flaws in the moral fiber of the larger society or culture.

Character educators do give a passing recognition to the complexity of the problems discussed. For example, they sometimes refer to the problems as "social pathologies" or "cultural ills." Nevertheless, they still oversimplify complex issues by making an easy and direct connection between social problems and individual morality. Lickona (1993) states, "As we confront the causes of our deepest societal problems...questions of character loom large" (p. 11). The fact is that they focus on the question of personal character and even magnify it while simultaneously casting a blind eye toward the fundamental socioeconomic causes of the problems. They never provide a thorough analysis of these social and cultural roots.

It is not an issue of deciding whether violence or drug abuse is a social problem or an individual problem but about understanding how the broader economic and social structure affects individual behavior and morality. It is not a matter of assigning a percentage of blame—for example, 35 percent individual and 65 percent social. The problems are predominantly and fundamentally rooted in sociocultural and economic causes. Moral poverty results from the lack of power—political, economic, and cultural power. Being marginalized, being victims of economic displacement and environmental racism, seriously damages personal development and well-being. How can moral life flourish amid the chemical refuse of corporate capitalism in East St. Louis? The hopelessness is rooted in powerlessness.

Root Causes of Youth Problems

Character educators' claim of moral decline reflects a particular view of youth and society. To deconstruct such a view and its root ideology, we need to conduct a historical and sociocultural analysis and situate problems among youth such as violence and drug abuse within the complex relationships between self and society, youth and adult, agency and control, and power and structure. We have to uncover the multiple layers and complex dimensions of the problems and demythologize many popular claims and ideologies. We need to address the fundamental societal problems underpinning youth problems and expose the ideological frameworks supporting common rationales for character education.

As argued earlier, even if we agree with character educators that there are indeed serious problems such as crime, violence, and drug abuse, we cannot uncritically accept the easy and direct connection they make between these problems and personal morality. The problems are too complex in their nature. Is there really moral deterioration in our society? Or is it just a convenient excuse for the promulgation of character education programs? Moreover, are there other political agendas involved in the popular claim of "moral deterioration"? We can deepen our understanding of these questions through a sociocultural analysis that is rarely found in the writings of character education leaders.

The Immediate Environment of Child Development
In order to better understand the problems of youth, we must look critically at the environment. As Cornell University psychologist James Garbarino (1995) points out, we are "raising children in a socially toxic environment." The toxic factors come from the immediate environment and the larger social

Moral Decline and Character Education

and cultural context. We need to investigate each of these factors. This section looks at the immediate environmental factors such as family, television, video games, and the Internet.

We may all agree that family and adults are critical in the development of children and adolescents, but now new technologies and the entertainment industry, combined with changes in family structure, have virtually isolated grown-ups from children and teenagers. Increasingly, children live without adults. The concerns over how children grow up in America have now entered the popular mainstream culture and appeared in popular news magazines such as *Time* and *Newsweek*. The youth culture is well captured in a feature article, "The Secret Life of Teens," in the May 10, 1999, issue of *Newsweek*. As the author, John Leland, warns us: "With as many as 11 million teenagers now online, more and more of adolescent life is taking place in a landscape that is inaccessible to many parents" (p. 45).

Kids now have less access to parents but more access to potentially damaging information from the media and the entertainment industry. The Internet, video games, and no-holds-barred music are creating new worlds for the young people that adults cannot enter. Parents do not often mediate and discuss with kids what is found online. When the teens are online, they are unsupervised, looking at whatever they please. They send emails and hang around chat rooms, where they encounter both adults and other teens and all the possibilities available on the Internet. They might even click on "The Anarchist Cookbook," a notorious handbook that includes instructions for building bombs. They can get everything from the Internet that they cannot get in their real life.

Video games are fraught with violence. Many kids are familiar with Half-Life, a multiplayer "first-person-shooter" (FPS) game. As Robert (the character in the game) pushes a key, a red shell fires from an on-screen shotgun; arms fly off, blood spatters on the wall. The best-known FPS game is Doom, a game reportedly favored by the shooters in Littleton, Colorado. The game Kingpin is described as a "multiplayer gang bang death match for up to 16 thugs!" according to its advertisement copy. Such games "target specific body parts and [one can] actually see the damage done including exit wounds" (in Leland, 1999, p. 48).

Violent video games are widespread. According to Leland, "The video-game business last year topped $6.3 billion....The more violent games are marked for sales to mature buyers only, but like R-rated movies, they are easily accessible to kids" (p. 48). Kids are living with violence. "We see so much violence on TV and in the movies that it just seems like it's everywhere. We don't go to school thinking we're going to be killed. But maybe it's because we're so used to it," says a fourteen-year-old boy in California (Leland, 1999, p. 48).

Parental supervision amid such a flood of new technologies and entertainment seems limited. Parents do not or are unable to set limits on their kids' pop-cultural diets. The pop-culture industry, marketing tribal styles through MTV and the Internet, makes it harder for parents to understand their kids than ever before. It is not surprising that many parents cannot read the densely encrypted messages and camp nihilism of Eminem, Marilyn Manson, or DMX. However, their kids may. Even if they cannot, these images and messages simply increase the interest in a world they cannot understand. In short, today's popular culture is quite complex and contains many counter-developmental influences. It is within this environment that our children construct a moral world.

According to child psychologists, there are some basic needs essential to development and well-being—the need for stability, security, affirmation and acceptance, family time, values and connection to community, and access to basic resources. But today's toxic environment often fails to meet these needs. It is difficult to grow up today. Children are living with more psychological maltreatment, including rejection, terror, and corruption. When their fathers disappear from their lives after separation and divorce, many children feel rejected. Children also feel cast off when parents cannot spend time with them. They are likely to be exposed to traumatic terror at the movies or at home watching TV. They are titillated by the sexuality that pervades the images on television and movies. They are desensitized to aggression by the ceaseless violence of video games that washes over them (Garbarino, 1995, p. 39).

As character educators tell us, many children display signs of serious problems such as a tendency to violence and drug abuse. However, this does not mean that the troubled kids are morally corrupt. Rather, such telltale signs inform us that their developmental environment is deteriorating and that they are vulnerable to the negative influence of such an environment. Instead of saying that our children are morally corrupt, we need to ask how many problems we as adults have created in the society and how the corruption in the adult world has harmed our children.

Character educators do recognize and even emphasize the toxic immediate environment of children such as dysfunctional families and violence-

Moral Decline and Character Education

fraught television programs, but they define this environment exclusively in terms of morality—moral decay has caused the deterioration of the environment. It is unacceptable to blame individuals, even children indirectly, as the ones who have created these problems. In actuality, children and youth are nothing but victims of a socially toxic environment.

Furthermore, we must place the immediate environment into a larger social and cultural context which constitutes the fundamental root causes of youth problems. Character educators never inform us about this important fact, but as we have seen, the environmental deterioration is inextricably linked to commercialism, to the marketplace, to the very free market enterprise system that character education leaders such as William Bennett advocate. The reality is that the laissez-faire approach of the marketplace may lead to a lack of social responsibility and morality. The epidemic of violent video games has been driven by the profit-seeking corporate system that exploits our children and undermines their moral lives.

The Larger Social and Cultural Contexts of Youth Problems

As stated earlier in this chapter, character educators de-emphasize the role of poverty and racism in crime and violence. Contrary to their arguments, we must call attention to the larger sociocultural contexts that determine the creation, production, and spread of problems such as violence among youth. Spina (2000) argues that the most commonly identified causes of violence, such as the deterioration of the nuclear family and TV violence, can almost be ignored when compared with more determining sociocultural factors. We cannot ignore the negative influences of the immediate environment on youth, but we must go further to examine the deeply rooted causes of youth problems. Violence in the media, inadequate parental supervision, and lack of religious upbringing are important issues, but we should not allow them to divert our attention from the more fundamental causes of violence. In the next four sections, I will examine several key issues related to the larger sociocultural context of youth problems—cultural support for violence, the gun culture, poverty, and the school practices that promote problems.

The Cultural Support for Violence. As Spina (2000) states, school violence

> is just one manifestation of a chronic, systemic, lethal disease both reinforced and hidden by a national ethos that romanticizes our violent past, deifies science, and celebrates aggression in business, books, sports, entertainment, domestic govern-

ment, and foreign policy, while letting it shape our future. (p. xv)

Watch *The Jerry Springer Show* or professional wrestling on television, and you will realize how deeply violence is embedded in the media as a reflection of the American life style. The raw violence and nastiness pervading these programs are shocking to visitors to this country. A virus has been unleashed within the culture, and too many young people are susceptible to it. As these programs demonstrate, violence is glorified and becomes entertainment. What is more disturbing is the enthusiasm and excitement the crowd shows at the overt display of raw violence.

Violence is promoted on television. Violence sells. Profit-making drives violence-fraught television programs. "Free" society has created the freedom in the marketplace, with mergers, acquisitions, and private parties competing. Narrow-minded and self-serving commercialism and consumerism dominate popular culture. The bottom line is that corporate power controls television, popular culture, and the public interest.

These television programs evidently reinforce values that promote violence. As Rich and DeVitis (1992) point out, "A pervasive characteristic of American life is its competitiveness" (p. 6). Competition is highly valued in American society and can be found in the daily functioning of various institutions and organizations. Although American society has become filled with assembly-line workers and Organization Men in whom functionalism reigns supreme, and individuals are required to get along with one another to be part of the corporate machine, competition, rather than harmony and peace, is the primary principle of interpersonal relations. The cowboy ethic and frontier ethos, both entangled with rugged survivalism as well as economic competition and social Darwinism, are central tenets of the American belief system. The competition-driven culture tends to view violence as an inevitable and normal part of human relations.

The cultural support for violence is, arguably, reflected in U.S. foreign policy. Using violence to conquer is rooted in U.S. imperialist policies of the nineteenth century and the historic claim of Manifest Destiny as imperialism swept from shore to shore, destroying races and the environment in its path. Contemporary U.S. foreign policy seems to apply a tortured, conflicted approach—inevitable tension arises among democratic impulses, cultural imperialism, and corporate imperatives. On the one hand, we have seen the post–World War II Marshall Plan, efforts to support emerging democracies (largely driven by American self-interest), Carter's Camp David accords, and

Clinton's Ireland peace initiative. On the other hand, the world has witnessed the United States' far-flung corporate, governmental, and imperialist intervention in the affairs of many countries.

Military intervention has become a norm in U.S. international relations. Especially since the Cold War ended and the United States became the single military superpower in the world, the U.S. government has frequently projected its power militarily and used violence to deal with international crises. From the Gulf War to the Kosovo crisis to "the war on terrorism," in the eyes of many international observers as well as the most outspoken American critics of U.S. foreign policy (see Noam Chomsky, 1999, 2000, 2001, for example), the U.S. government has helped to create a more violent world and to establish that violence is a legitimate way of problem-solving.

The most recent United States–led wars in Afghanistan (2001) and Iraq (2003), coming after the atrocious 9/11 terrorist attacks, have received strong support from much of the American public. But one essential aspect of the wars, civilian casualties, was veiled by the American government and mainstream media and therefore excluded from the public's concern. According to many independent surveys, the civilian death toll in Afghanistan surpassed casualties from 9/11 (Gonzalez, 2002), and the total number of reported civilian deaths in the Iraq war and occupation was well above 8,000 by the end of November 2003 (www.iraqbodycount.net). However, such tremendous loss of human life has not received the American people's condolence and sympathy (in large part because it has been so little reported on or analyzed).

As a result of government propaganda and the media's biased coverage, much of the American public has turned a blind eye to the savage killing of innocent people outside of the United States. Fueled by a cultural value, namely, addressing intolerable injustice with violence, many did not bother to critically consider the logic of the "war on terror" and its potential consequences. Few Americans seemed to understand that retaliation only generates more hatred, and killing will only cause more terrorism.

That militarism has become a ready tool of corporate interests and that violence has been embraced by U.S. foreign policy may be disputable points, but they still raise a concern for the analysis of character education. We must consider the possibility that socially sanctioned violence—military adventures, national wars, and capital punishment, to name a few of examples—contributes to a wider and deeper acceptance of violence in other spheres. When the American president declared a U.S. victory in the war against Iraq from the dramatic setting of the nuclear-powered aircraft carrier *U.S.S.*

Abraham Lincoln and when Jeb Bush addressed the National Rifle Association and cheered "The sound of our guns is the sound of freedom," we know what kind of message our leaders are sending to the world and to our own children. Support for violence represents a serious sociocultural risk. One group who will most likely take the risk is youth. As Garbarino (1999) points out, the lost boys who have killed others have internalized the typical American cultural value that embraces violence to fight for justice. He notes, "In our society the idea of retribution through violence is a basic article of faith. Vengeance is not confined to some small group of psychologically devastated individuals. It is normal for us, a fact of value in our culture" (p. 133). Youth become the victims of this violent culture. As the most vulnerable members of our community, they show us where the negative values in our culture lead. They show us how things really are on the fringe.

The Epidemic of Guns. The proponents of character education often cite youth violence, especially school shootings, as a sign of moral decline or character decay. However, they do not closely examine the gun culture in America, the context of gun violence. Supported by a culture of violence, many Americans are obsessed with weapons. Any person from a country in which guns are strictly confined to a small number of citizens and the gun crime rate is extremely low finds it easy to connect the epidemic of violence in the United States with the epidemic of guns. America's gun laws are porous, and children and youth have too easy an access to guns.

Andrew Murr (1999) of *Newsweek* traced the guns used in the Columbine High School massacre and found that under Colorado law, Eric Harris and Dylan Klebold could own rifles and shotguns but were too young to buy them. However, they had an eighteen-year-old friend do the buying, and she purchased two shotguns and a 9-mm Hi-point carbine for them. Their other weapon was a pistol, a type of handgun that, according to both state and federal laws, they were unable to either buy or own.

The four guns, Murr told us, were all from the Tanner Gun Show, an event that fills the Denver Merchandise Mart nine times a year. There are more than four thousand gun shows a year in the United States, and this is where gun control regulations break down. Gun shows routinely rent space to private sellers who are not covered by the law and who do not make the required background checks. A 1999 report by the U.S. Department of Justice estimated that felons illegally bought weapons at gun shows in 46 percent of the 314 cases studied and concluded that gun shows involve "a disturbing pattern" of criminal activity.

Stricter gun control would obviously be beneficial for our kids but has been difficult to legislate. The gun trade is a huge business. Gun control means less profit, and, of course, this is not in the interest of the National Rifle Association (NRA) and others who have benefited from the gun industry. It is not surprising that NRA advocates are against gun control, but it is strange that some character education proponents de-emphasize its importance. In March 2001, students were shot in schools in California and Pennsylvania, including a suburban San Diego high school where two students were killed and thirteen other people wounded. After the incident, Secretary of Education Rod Paige said that student "alienation and rage" is the biggest factor in school shootings and that addressing that problem, rather than changing gun laws, should be the country's priority.

Paige said guns cannot be at fault because there have been reports of students plotting violence with bombs and other devices. "We think just focusing on guns is much too narrow, it is beyond guns. The guns may be the instrument of the violence, but they are not the cause of the violence," Paige said on CNN's *Late Edition*. Paige recommended more after-school programs, parental involvement, and character education. He said the Bush's administration wanted to expand character education and wanted religion-based organizations to participate in the after-school programs.

Paige's de-emphasis of gun control and recommendation of character education are problematic. In order to address the shootings, we cannot ignore the psychological crises of some young people, and we have no reason to focus on gun control alone. However, we cannot simply overlook the fact that young people today live in a culture in which guns are endemic and easily obtainable. It is logical to say that if we have fewer guns, we will have less gun violence. Can we blame the six-year-old boy who shot his classmate, a six-year-old girl, and expand character education in kindergarten classrooms in response? In January 2002, an eleven-year-old boy in Hamilton, New York, accidentally killed his playmate, a thirteen-year-old boy. Can we focus on the "alienation and rage" and not ask how the boy had access to the gun? We can only be outraged by the reality that guns are out of control and our children are in danger. In many situations, the issue of character development is simply not a factor, and character education is not the answer.

The issue is not "alienation and rage" vs. guns. In most cases, it was alienation and rage *combined with* easy access to guns that killed so many. While emphasizing character education, Paige and other decision-makers fail to analyze why there is so much alienation and rage among our young people. When they prescribe character education as a panacea, they ignore the reality our youngsters are facing every day: large-scale, impersonal, bureaucratic schools; excessive high-stakes testing; a curriculum and teachers that do not care about children; and a youth culture that permits cliques and gangs. Throw guns into that mix, and it can become explosive.

Paige's "alienation and rage" focus is largely left at the individual level. He does not call for school restructuring, which is needed to fundamentally address alienation and rage among youth. Locating the problem within the individual without addressing overall school structure and culture only reinforces the isolation of the individual and creates more alienation and rage.

We have to address the issues surrounding guns and gun control, especially the larger economic and political issues. The gun industry is an integral part of the corporate economy. The NRA advocates not only unrestricted weapon ownership but also a free-market economy. Gun control threatens the economic power of the NRA and its allies. The deadly school shootings have shocked these people because perhaps the next time their own kids will be involved. However, self-interest has driven them to look at other solutions than gun control, such as addressing the "alienation and rage" issue first. It is not difficult to decipher the priorities and politics of the power elite like Rod Paige and his boss. We have to understand the limitations of their prescriptions. The epidemic of guns and gun violence is largely a structural problem; accordingly, structural change is needed to solve the problem.

Poverty. Earlier in this chapter, I questioned character educators' de-emphasis of economic poverty as a cause of crime and argued that poverty indeed has significantly contributed to youth problems. I want to stress here that the economic conditions American children face today are much worse than in many other countries and have seriously worsened. According to a 2003 update from Columbia University's National Center for Children in Poverty (NCCP), "The United States child poverty rate is substantially higher—often two-to-three times higher—than that of most other major Western industrialized nations" (Lu, 2003). The federal poverty level for a two-parent family of four in 2001 was $17,960. NCCP reports:

> 16% of American children—almost 12 million—lived in poverty in 2001, meaning their parents' income was at or below the federal poverty level. 7% of American children—5 million—lived in extreme poverty in 2001. This was a 17% increase

from 2000. The parents of these children made half the federal poverty level. (Lu, 2003)

Earlier in this chapter, we challenged the validity of many statistics used by character education leaders. We can still question the statistics on children in poverty here, however, as Morse (2003) states, "the 'official' poverty rate is high enough, but the unofficial one is even higher" (p. 26). The problems related to child poverty are universally acknowledged. An NCCP spokesperson, Jamie Hickner, deplored the child poverty situation:

> There has been ample research that shows that poverty hurts young children the most. Poverty on children is devastating; it has an enormous impact on their psychological and physiological development. Childhood poverty has been very strongly correlated to high infant mortality, to the likelihood of experiencing violence during childhood and suffering from domestic violence, and to difficulties obtaining full-time employment. It is very depressing to think that this is well known and well documented, yet the problem still persists. (in Scherrer, 1998)

When hunger and impoverishment become everyday matters for children and young adults, violence and drug dealing and abuse come as no surprise. In a country considered one of the richest in the world, poverty can be largely explained as relative deprivation. When relative deprivation is as serious as the top 1 percent of the population holding 46.2 percent of all stocks and 54.2 percent of all bonds (Giroux, 1997, p. 39), poverty or deprivation is deeply tied to inequality and injustice. Inequality and injustice produce anger and conflict.

The sociological explanation of youth deviance makes sense here. The economic structure has produced a stratified society in which the system dictates goals for success for all citizens, but institutional access is limited to primarily the middle and upper strata. Lower- and working-class individuals are systematically excluded from the competition. Some members of the lower class retaliate by choosing a deviant alternative. When socially sanctioned means are not available for the realization of highly desirable goals, the only way to achieve the goals is to detour around them and bypass the approved means. For young people raised in urban ghettos with poor housing facilities, dilapidated schools, and inadequate family and community life, their road to success is more likely to deviate from the normative route of school and hard work.

It needs to be noted that it is stereotypical and racist to connect drug dealing, pimping, and theft with poor kids in urban ghettos. "Black urban pimps" is a dangerous illusion. In reality, many urban youth strive to succeed and many do make it, albeit in difficult circumstances. It is the hard-core, truly alienated groups that usually get involved in drug dealing and street crimes. Nevertheless, many deviant behaviors result from the lack of access to culturally prescribed goals and the lack of legitimate means for attaining these goals. Contrary to the claims of character education leaders, such as William Bennett, a structural lack of opportunities is the main cause of deviance and crime, not individual pathology.

School Practices That Create and Reinforce Youth Problems. Economic inequality is reflected in American schools. The "savage inequalities" (Kozol, 1992) in the public education system are mainly caused by the shocking differences in educational spending between wealthy suburban schools and poor inner-city schools. Because efforts to radically reform school funding have not been found to produce structural changes in the system, the conditions in the schools our poor children attend will remain unchanged for many years to come. It is not surprising that in many poor, predominantly minority-populated schools, we find overcrowded, underheated classrooms without enough textbooks or qualified teachers.

Along with poverty, racism is embedded in schools and schooling. The Supreme Court decision *Brown vs. Board of Education,* in which the Court found segregated education unconstitutional, has not produced the integration in public schooling that its advocates envisioned. Racially segregated schooling is a reality for today's children in so many schools. Most of the urban schools Kozol visited, for example, were 95 percent to 99 percent nonwhite. In addition, within many schools, the prevailing tracking system is extremely racist. As Kozol (1992) reports:

> Classes for the emotionally handicapped, neurologically impaired, learning disabled and educable mentally retarded are disproportionately black....Citywide fewer than 10 percent of children slotted in these special tracks will graduate from school. Nationwide, black children are three times as likely as white children to be placed in classes for the mentally retarded but only half as likely to be placed in classes for the gifted. (p. 119)

Ten years later, similar trends in schools remain. Black students are still less likely to be placed in gifted and talented programs and more likely to be in

Moral Decline and Character Education 91

special education programs (see Toppo, 2001 and The Harvard Civil Rights project, 2002, for statistics and reports on racial inequity in special education). As Berlak (2002) reports:

> African-Americans are 4.5 times as likely to be in schools that rank low in math and twice as likely to be in schools that rank low in reading. In addition, 6.9% of students of color are identified for gifted programs compared to 23% of white students.

Such statistics have aroused a sense of shame and anger in many readers, but more shameful is the fact that similar outrage is rarely heard from the power elite. Many kids indeed survive the lower track, and some eventually shine in academics and other areas. But in many schools the tracking system works to sort out kids, not academically but racially and socioeconomically. Kids on the lower tracks suffer neglect from the very beginning and most likely lose opportunities to learn and succeed forever.

Institutional and systematic racism is endemic to tracking. As Fine (1997) argues, whiteness is produced through tracking as advantage/merit, and racism is created and enforced in schools. She describes the "unfortunately predictable" racial splitting by track in a high school—how tracking is not determined by academic merit but by race:

> Students have what is considered a race-neutral "choice" about which track they opt into. And they "chose" by race. White racism here—and elsewhere—is so thoroughly institutionalized and embodied that young people, when given an opportunity, "choose" their "place," and seemingly with little protest. (p. 59)

Children in these schools, and not only the minority kids, are suffering every day from an unjust and morally deplorable system. How can we manage to teach them justice and morality? However, none of the national reports and reform proposals made even passing reference to problems such as racial segregation. Low reading scores, high dropout rates, poor motivation, and other symptoms seemed to dominate the discussion (e.g., Bennett and Wynne's effective schools formula). Accordingly, the reform proposals focus on setting higher academic standards and reinforcing character education. These children do not need moral education. The educational and social systems are morally corrupt and need radical reform.

Poor and racist schools help produce youth problems such as violence and teen pregnancies. At East St. Louis High School, a pregnant teenage girl told people: "There is no reason not to have a baby. There's not much for me in public school" (Kozol, 1992, p. 29). A diploma from a ghetto high school does not count for much in the United States. The girls and boys there do not have a future and do not have much self-esteem. As another young black man at a Washington, D.C., high school stated: "Well, we supposed to be stupid…we perform poorly in school cause we got it all thought up in our heads that we're supposed to be dumb so we might as well go ahead and be dumb" (Berlak, 2002). Knowing that they are written off by their society, these kids have no feeling of belonging to their community and country. "Gangs provide the boys, perhaps, with something to belong to" (Kozol, 1992, p. 34).

Many school practices help create and reinforce youth problems. As introduced earlier, Secretary of Education Rod Paige blamed "alienation and rage" among youth for school shootings and urged character education, faith-based programs, and parental involvement to solve the problem. Paige failed to address the fundamental problems. For example, the administration he serves strongly promotes controversial educational policies requiring higher academic standards and more high-stakes tests for students. As many have convincingly argued, academic competition in the form of high-stakes testing causes many problems (Kohn, 1992, 2000; Rich & DeVitis, 1992). It incites cheating and other dishonest activities, stimulates rivalry, envy, and distrust, and engenders stress, despair, and shame in defeat. All of these could lead to alienation and rage among students. Even if character education were expanded in schools and religious organizations and parents became more involved, as long as these efforts are not expected to challenge the competition-driven educational policy, it is unlikely that they will bring any significant changes to the youth culture.

Failing to address fundamental structural problems in schools and harmful educational policies, character educators stress individual morality. The notion gets promoted that if young people fail, it is due to something within them. This has been perfectly demonstrated by the story of Joe Clark, a former high school principal in New Jersey. Former Education Secretary William Bennett called Clark's school "a Mecca of education" and paid tribute to Joe Clark for throwing out three hundred students who were thought to be involved with violence or drugs. (According to Kozol [1992], two thirds of the kids that Clark threw out ended up in Passaic County Jail.) Clark was touted as a hero, especially for black people. He was on the cover of *Time* magazine. In addition to throwing out troubled kids, Clark devoutly embraced Bennett's moral education scheme. Clark repeatedly called for values such as self-control, discipline, and respect for authority to be imposed on his students. On the day Bennett made his visit to the school, Clark came out and walked the hallways with a bullhorn and a bat. He did not look like a school principal but the warden of a jail.

Psychology of Adolescence:
Youth Problems as Responses to Social Toxicity

We realize that today's children and youth inhabit a socially and culturally toxic environment. Many negative factors complicate their moral, emotional, and social development and create deviance and serious problems. However, to understand why problems occur, we need to conduct a psychological analysis. After all, negative environments do not cause all people in those environments to kill. Character education is, largely, a psychologically based approach, but it is exclusively centered on personal character or individual morality and is, consequently, problematic. A broader and deeper psychological analysis of youth and their problems will help us understand the weakness in character educators' analysis.

Psychologists tell us that youth problems such as violent crimes and drug abuse are largely responses to sociocultural toxicity. Youth living in a socially toxic environment often take risks to be deviant and become rule-breakers. According to Ponton's (1999) analysis, all adolescents are going to take risks. Under materially or psychologically difficult circumstances, adolescents tend to identify themselves through rebellion and anger at parents or other adults and engage in high-risk behaviors including drinking, smoking, drug use, reckless driving, unsafe sexual activity, eating disorders, self-mutilation, stealing, gang activity, and violence.

Many other research findings also show us how isolation, rejection, neglect, depression, shame, and struggle have been woven into the inner world of youth and created killers and criminals. Shockley (2001) indicates that even if the social matrix of the suburbs is different from that of inner-city neighborhoods, some white kids from the wealthy suburbs may manifest the same psychological problems and engage in the same behavior.

Earlier in this chapter, Garbarino's (1995) analysis of how children today live in a "socially toxic environment" was introduced. In another influential book, *Lost Boys: Why Our Sons Turn Violent and How We Can Save Them*, he powerfully argues that boys who have been psychologically abused by the adult world end up as killers. Garbarino (1999) argues that many people do not really want to understand the dangers that such boys face or to try to make sense of how their violent acts flow from their experiences in our society.

Character educators view young killers as morally corrupt and assume that moral poverty has caused them to kill. As we remember, Bennett and Lickona tell many stories about youth crimes. They describe the cruelty of young killers; the crimes are grandiose, egotistical, and arrogant. Young killers seem to easily take a human life just because they feel insulted, frustrated, or teased, or simply because they need money. Reading these descriptions, we naturally think they are rotten kids. However, Garbarino (1999) warns us: "There is much more to the story....Rarely do we hear of inquiries into their emotional lives or of efforts to make sense of their acts. Why is that?" (p. 3). We have to look at their actions and the scope of their moral framework and ask how their moral sense is being lost in the world.

Most of the lost boys do have a moral framework, albeit a damaged one. The boys are often lost themselves in the world of killings and cannot make sense of what they did. It is difficult even for adults in our violent world to draw the line and determine which killings are justified and which are not. In a society where bombing, killing, terrorist attacks, and retaliation are all present, how can we expect children and youth to always draw clear lines in their conceptions and actions? They are living in a morally confusing world, and it is not surprising that they become confused, especially when they are controlled by narrow and intense personal needs. Garbarino (1999) reports that most news reports paint young killers as ungrateful or crazed monsters, but further investigation often reveals that the killings took place after years of deteriorating relationships and, most often, abuse. He points out an important fact:

> Almost all acts of violence are related to perceived injustice, the subjective experience of frustrated justice, and an attempt to redress injustice. Deadly petulance usually hides some deep emotional wounds, a way of compensating through an exaggerated sense of grandeur for an inner sense of violation, victimization, and injustice. (p. 128)

We must keep these complicated situations in mind as we look deeper into the stories of young people who kill. We must walk a bit in the lost boys' shoes before we judge them. The violence that lost boys commit does not necessarily indicate a total moral breakdown. More often, the violence committed has its source in their own ideas of "morality." This point is important because we must look beyond our shock, horror, and indignation to see the roots of the problem. Before we begin to blame the killers, before we impose any moral instruction programs on them, we must examine their inner worlds and their damaged moral systems.

We as adults must protect boys, and girls, from negative "moral development" and teach them moral behavior. We must develop empathy in them and protect them from degrading, dehumanizing, and desensitizing images. We need to nurture the spiritual development of children. We must provide care and encourage caring. Unfortunately, as we will see in later chapters, these elements are inadequately presented in the proposals of character educators, who impose external rules and traditional values without carefully considering children's inner needs and making connections to the children's environment.

Clearly, character educators do not attempt to conduct such in-depth analysis on why young people commit violence and what has caused them to kill. They do not look deeply into children's inner worlds, nor do they extensively check the external environment children live within. That there is something wrong with their morality becomes a convenient answer. That may be true, but the morality does not develop in a vacuum. Obviously, the moral deterioration identified by character educators results from something other than children's lack of character. Perhaps the real causes lie in the exploitation and oppression in their lives and the resulting alienation from the self and others.

Moral Decline and the Legitimating of Socialization

Character educators have largely targeted youth as the scapegoats for social problems. This last section of the chapter examines how targeting youth and blaming them for social problems leads to the very core of character educators' scheme—socialization.

Blaming Youth for Social Problems

Henry Giroux (1997, 2000) examines how media, politicians, and intellectuals censure youth and how violence and sex are used to shroud the victimization of youth. He argues that popular culture, represented by Hollywood films and other mainstream media, presents youth as a social disorder and a menace. In these films and other media images, "youth are increasingly defined through the lens of contempt or criminality" (Giroux, 2000, p. 94). For example, in many Hollywood films, such as *Dumb and Dumber* (1994) and *Kids* (1996), teenagers are portrayed as vulgar, disengaged pleasure-seekers, and over-the-edge violent sociopaths. They are decadent, drug-crazed, pathological, and criminal. In a word, youth are demonized.

Youth are also commodified or constructed as consuming subjects. Advertising (for example, Calvin Klein's ads) targets youth as commodities. In these popular narratives, "one-dimensional and ahistorical representations of youth erase the complexities and contradictions of place, style, language, and individual histories" (Giroux, 1997, p. 24). Missing from the media portrait is any mention of power, ideology, and human rights. Also absent is any challenge to the exploitation and domination youth suffer.

To make the situation worse, politicians and some intellectuals have used the popular cultural image to wage more assaults against youth. In their view, youth become symbols of aberrant promiscuity, social degeneracy, and moral decay. Youth are accused of leading the country into moral decline and tearing the fabric of the nation asunder. The critique by the leaders of character education has been an integral part of this popular narrative. Their sweeping views have fooled the more uncritical public, including teachers, into believing the dark view of youth.

Setting up youth as scapegoats resonates with political and economic policies which harm youth.

> As the discourse on youth shifts from an emphasis on social failing in the society to questions of individual character, social policy moves from the language of social investment—creating safety nets for children—to the language of containment and blame. (Giroux, 1997, p. 17)

Bennett (1994) and Bennett, Dilulio, and Walters (1996) argue that social investment is not needed. Instead of talking about eradicating poverty, building decent schools, and creating viable jobs, Bennett and other conservative commentators either invoke the punitive demand for more prisons or emphasize Victorian moralism.

In character educators' portraits, young people are no longer seen as a symptom of a wider social dilemma; they are the problem. For example, character educators always criticize the sexualization of youth in Hollywood movies, but they simply blame youth for sexual acts. And by such criticism, they send the simplistic message that sex is bad. Thus, abstinence-based sex

Moral Decline and Character Education 97

education has been integrated into the character education movement (Lickona, 1993). Many such programs spread fear and misinformation with grotesque and terrifying imagery, portraying teenage sexuality as decadent and predatory and urging teens to simply say no to sex. These strategies do not prepare teens to deal with their own emerging sexuality. They lack a genuine respect for and understanding of young people and fail to establish a connection between youth and the social context. The effectiveness of these programs is limited.

Character educators portray kids as if they live in a historical, political, and cultural vacuum without memory or history. They provide no larger context for understanding the cultural, social, and institutional forces on their lives. Violence, drugs, and sexuality are portrayed as personal choices. In reality, violence, drugs, and sexuality may constitute the daily experience of young people who live in places that foster suffering and oppression. Violence, drugs, and sex may be part of their everyday struggle. Even in affluent communities, many children of the rich, the powerful, and the famous are left free to experiment. They have more than they need or want and resort to seeking pleasure in alienated lives. Like the poor kids, they are culturally and socially impoverished.

Giroux and other critical theorists envision a cultural pedagogy for educators. Giroux (1997) argues:

> Young people need to become critical agents able to recognize, appropriate, and transform how dominant power works on and through them. To achieve this, they need forms of educational practice steeped in respectful selfhood that do not collapse social into personal problems or systematic oppression into the language of victim-blaming. In short, they need a pedagogy that provides the basis for improvisation and responsible resistance. (p. 32)

Character education, which stems from the larger political agenda that blames youth, can hardly offer anything consistent with such a pedagogy. Its emphasis on individual morality can hardly engage youth and redirect their social practices and activities.

Character Education for Socialization

Defining youth as behaviorally deviant and morally corrupt naturally leads to character educators' next claim: Children and youth need to be socialized to the established rules and standards of society. The socialization of youth is thus legitimated as the central goal of character education.

Politicians (such as American presidents) have always seen schools as the moral underpinning of the nation. Theodore Roosevelt's statement "To educate a person in mind and not in morals is to educate a menace to society" has become one of the most popular slogans of the current character education movement (see Lickona, 1993). The 2002 White House conference on character education strongly stressed the link between character education and national service, recommending both military service and service as "citizen soldiers," which combines military and civilian forms of service. At the conference, Secretary of State Colin Powell emphasized character education as the means of imposing the values of the United States as a nation. Another keynote speaker, William Damon, urged educators to embrace the "transcendent purpose" of character education—patriotism.

The implications of these slogans, claims, or arguments are clear: Via moral/character education, schools are society's agents. Schools must transmit the knowledge and values that are produced by and support the established society and its existing political and economic systems. Education becomes socialization. Educators seek to socialize children to be productive, yet obedient, members of society. This approach has a long tradition, which advocates see as having philosophical support from theorists such as Aristotle and Durkheim and receiving the endorsement of the social elite, such as William Bennett, who benefit from the established power relations and, therefore, defend the status quo.

This tradition has caused the public to expect that schooling should enforce a moral code and act as an agent of stability to prevent delinquency even outside of school (Tyack, 1974; Tyack & Cuban, 1995). This expectation has been well integrated into educational policy-making throughout the history of American education. As we have seen, the nineteenth-century Common School was charged with the duty of assimilating poor immigrants from Europe and Asia (who were viewed as wild, prone to violence, and antisocial) into the American social order. In an 1881 report by the NEA, high schools were called "the most potential agency…to root up vice and to lessen crime" (Anderson, 1998, p. 317).

Throughout the 1960s and 1970s, when violence spread throughout American society, the expectation that schools should counter violence grew stronger. During the Johnson administration, the Commission of Law Enforcement and Administration of Justice stated that the school, "unlike the family, is a public instrument for training young people.…It is the principal public institution for development of basic commitment by young people to the goals and values of our society" (Anderson, 1998, p. 318). Obviously, today politicians such as Clinton and Bush and educators such as Ryan and Lickona have wholeheartedly embraced this long tradition and worked to strengthen the expectation that schools will eradicate social problems by socializing children.

When it comes to specific character education programs, we see a solid merger of citizenship education and character education. Again, this has an historical precedent. The growth of character education in the 1920s, as we examined in chapter 2, was largely the State's response, via the schools, to the declining ability of the church and the family to maintain the social order. The character education programs represented a State-sanctioned moral system. Worthy character was seen as the basis of good citizenship, and the school, through character education, had to produce good citizens for the State. The goal of the ideal society was ever present in character education programs. In the character traits or morality codes developed by character educators, social values took precedence over other values. The extended life-adjustment goals of character education were consistent with the maintenance of the social order.

Similarly, character education programs today emphasize citizenship education. Bill Clinton made no distinction between character education and citizenship education when he pledged his administration's support for the movement. While bemoaning the so-called moral decay in society and troubling youth behavior, character educators seem to be more worried about the possible decline of the Republic and the fall of American civilization than the well-being of children and youth. They put the nation's political and economic systems before the individual. The overwhelming emphasis of character education objectives is still on socially oriented values. For instance, the 2002 White House character education conference called special attention to concepts of civic duty and national service.

Citizenship education is thus promoted as mere socialization. The role of the individual as an active citizen and participant in the general polity is generally ignored. Society is promoted as having absolute authority, which is not subject to significant critique and challenge. Grumbling about the growing rejection by youth of the economic and political system, George W. Bush said at the 2002 White House character education conference: "Americans believe in character education because we want more for our children than apathy and cynicism." Colin Powell was even more direct in suggesting that questioning the government is as unacceptable as shaming one's family.

Character educators have established an uncritical definition of citizenship education. They agree with John Dewey in locating the individual's moral life within the social life and stressing the school's responsibility for advancing the welfare of society, but they overlook the fact that Dewey also wanted education, moral education in particular, to move beyond socialization. Dewey (1897/1974) argues that children must be educated for *democratic* citizenship. The child must be educated so that "he may take charge of himself; may not only adapt himself to the changes which are going on, but have power to shape and direct those changes" (p. 114).

Character educators certainly do not empower students to become critical citizens for social change. As Ryan (1989) states,

> Character development puts a heavy emphasis on culture. While it fully engages the transformational goal of schools, which is to make the student as an active agent in the positive transformation of society, it places more emphasis on the traditional role of the school as transmitter of the culture. (p. 14)

Thus, Ryan accepts the emphasis on transmission over transformation in character education. And the actual programs in character education do not show students transforming society but rather students conforming to institutional norms and values. Ryan further claims that the public pays teachers not to teach students to change the social order but to teach them to preserve it (p. 15). Thus, character educators certainly do not encourage critical thinking and even devalue the ability and skills needed to make ethical decisions. Again, enculturation and socialization of youth to the established economic, political, and social orders are legitimated.

Conclusion

I have suggested in this chapter that character education as an integral part of the 1980s school reform movement reflects the social and cultural contexts of the time and mirrors conservative sociopolitical policies. When capitalism faced a challenge, politicians and social elites asked schools to produce more productive yet obedient workers and citizens. By overestimating moral decline and character decay, the leaders of character education purposefully conceal the political and social nature of problems such as violence and drug

Moral Decline and Character Education 101

abuse. They overemphasize behavioral problems among youth and strengthen the role of the school to socialize children. This is the typical logic of character education crusaders: There is nothing wrong with the economic and political systems; there is only something wrong with people's character and morality. So do not attempt to make any structural change at the societal level; just work hard to perfect your individual morality. This logic represents and reinforces the interests of the people in power. Character education was politicized from its very beginning.

Keeping the political rationale for character education in mind, we will look into its theory and practice in the next two chapters. These chapters will argue that, consistent with its political agenda, the virtue-centered character education movement is deeply rooted in certain social and cultural traditions and carries particular political and ideological influences.

CHAPTER FOUR

Character Education in Theory: Moral Philosophies and Ideologies

The claim of moral decline, along with political and ideological needs, has driven the character education movement. This chapter will focus on theory and will critically examine the work of leading contemporary character education advocates and explore the political and ideological orientations embedded within the process of their theorizing. The analysis focuses on the works of William Bennett and Edwin Delattre (1978), William Bennett (1993), William Kilpatrick (1992), Edward Wynne (1989a, 1989b), Thomas Lickona (1991, 1993, 1998, 1999), and Kevin Ryan (1989). It then goes on to examine the commonalities of their theoretical claims and reveals their ideological assumptions.

Bennett, Kilpatrick, and Wynne: Establishing a Theoretical Framework

Modern character education proponents begin by attacking those moral education theories that had departed from the orthodox character education tradition. They condemn values clarification and the cognitive-developmental model as expressions of "the individualist spirit of the age" (Lickona, 1993) and as unreliable and misleading. Character educators advocate and advertise their own moral philosophy of traditional character education.

Bennett and Kilpatrick: Teaching Virtues, Training Behaviors, and Returning to Tradition

In their article in *The Public Interest,* William Bennett and Edwin Delattre (1978) open fire on values clarification and the cognitive-developmental approach to moral education. They argue that there is a serious lack of moral content in values clarification, which addresses desires, wants, likes, and dislikes but not values or morals. They also attack the moral relativism they found in that theory, believing that there are problems inherent in having no right or wrong answers to questions of morality and conduct.

Bennett and Delattre (1978) do not align Kohlberg's cognitive approach with moral relativism. They actually acknowledge his stress on certain values, such as justice and participatory democracy, and his recognition of educating students to be rational as a core of moral education; nevertheless, they reject Kohlberg's emphasis on individual rights and his de-emphasis on authority. Kohlberg's libertarian conception of moral judgment presumably involves respect for rights of all individuals, but Bennett and his coauthor consider this "a curious libertarianism" and impossible to realize. They call Kohlberg's theory "a particular ideology giving certain individuals and groups of individuals rights more than equal to those of others" (p. 97). Specifically, they criticize Kohlberg for favoring the disadvantaged: "The claims of those in authority and the claims of rules always yield to the claims of the 'disadvantaged'" (p. 97). They complain about the loss of the rights of authority in Kohlberg's approach and are discontented with a program advocating justice and fairness for all individuals, especially the disadvantaged and underprivileged.

Discarding the concept of rights stressed in Kohlberg's approach, Bennett and Delattre (1978) propose a different view of morality. They argue that "morality is concerned with doing good, with sacrifice, altruism, love, courage, honor, and compassion, and with fidelity and large-mindedness regarding one's station, commitments, family, friends, colleagues, and society in general" (p. 97). As I will discuss in the next chapter, these are the very traits that character educators promote.

Advocates for both values clarification and the cognitive-developmental approach criticize the dogmatic nature of traditional moral education. They embrace a liberal, democratic, and non-indoctrinating notion of education. Bennett and Delattre (1978) argue that both approaches fail to avoid indoctrination of values they consider important. Both approaches are denounced not for opposing indoctrination per se but for opposing the indoctrination of traditional values. There is no doubt that Bennett and Delattre want to convey the message that the indoctrination of traditional values is perfectly acceptable.

William Bennett's (1993) best-selling book, *The Book of Virtues: A Treasury of Great Moral Stories,* is a collection of stories that illustrate virtues, including self-discipline, loyalty, and faith. "The purpose of the book is to show parents, teachers, students, and children what the virtues look like, what they are in practice, how to recognize them, and how they work" (p. 11). The book has been a cornerstone of the new character education movement, and, as we shall see, character education programs in schools typically focus on a list of character traits that is similar to Bennett's list. The underlying philosophy of Bennett's approach is clearly stated in the book and is represented in many character education programs:

> Moral education—the training of heart and mind toward the good—involves many things. It involves rules and precepts—the dos and don'ts of life with others—as well as explicit instruction, exhortation, and training. Moral education must provide training in good habits. (p. 11)

Thus, moral education in Bennett's view does not value free choice or reasoning for decision-making as promoted by values clarification and the cognitive-developmental approach. Rather, it trains people to be good by prescribing rules and precepts and forming good habits. Exactly as James Terry White argued in 1909, Bennett uses examples in the formation of moral habits. For White and Bennett, the purpose of moral education is to train children in certain specific virtues. By being exposed to the great virtues as exemplified through role models, children are expected to identify, admire, and acquire these same virtues. Through practice, the virtues then become habitual, and the children eventually become virtuous themselves. It is obvious that in rejecting other moral education theories, Bennett and his followers promote an old notion of moral training, one which is narrowly defined and strikingly inadequate.

Another influential character education writer, William Kilpatrick (1992), overtly adopts the same conceptual framework in *Why Johnny Can't Tell Right from Wrong*, another well-publicized character education book. Like Bennett and Lickona, Kilpatrick draws on a series of statistics regarding "troubling youth behaviors" to conclude that youngsters today cannot tell right from wrong, and he blames schools for their failure in moral education. The failure of moral education, argues Kilpatrick, results from teaching "the wrong method" (p. 15), namely, values clarification and Kohlberg's cognitive-developmental approach.

Like Bennett, Kilpatrick laments that there is no "moral" in moral education curricula. Too much time and energy are spent exchanging opinions and exploring feelings, but no time is given to providing moral guidance or forming character.

> The virtues are not explained or discussed, no models of good behavior are provided, no reason is given why a boy or girl should want to be good in the first place. In short, students are given nothing to live by or look up to. (p. 22)

Kilpatrick's model of moral education is the same as Bennett's: setting examples of virtues and cultivating virtues. He acknowledges the concern of proponents of values clarification and the moral reasoning approach regarding the misuse of traditional moral education methods such as using songs, films, marches, and myths as tools of indoctrination. However, he discredits the teaching of critical thinking and rational strategies in those approaches:

> It is mistaken. History strongly suggests that the dream of a rational morality or a rational society is always just that—a dream; a dream, moreover, that can easily turn into a nightmare, creating systems and societies just as inhuman as the ones they are meant to avoid. (p. 24)

Kilpatrick (1992) realizes the potential of those approaches to produce individuals with greater political and social awareness. Yet, he believes that political and social awareness is simply not as important as personal character and integrity.

Morality, argues Kilpatrick, has little to do with children's feelings or difficult ethical problems but has much to do with behavior. He believes that "most of our 'moral decisions' have to do with temptations to do things we know we shouldn't do or temptations to avoid doing the things we know we should do" (p. 85). Based on this observation, he further claims in an extremely assertive manner: "The hard part of morality, in short, is not knowing what is right but doing it. And if this is so, the remedy lies not in forming opinions but in forming good habits" (p. 88).

Kilpatrick (1992) uses Plato and Aristotle to support his claim that reason and reasoning are not important in moral education. He cites Plato's belief that young minds are like young puppies and would only "pull and tear at arguments" (p. 89). It is much more important for children to learn to love virtue than to argue about it. Morality, argues Kilpatrick, requires acquaintance with "moral premises" (p. 94). He also contends that "moral premises are not reasoned to but are seen or grasped by an intuitive act. And being able to grasp them, as Aristotle suggested, may well be a factor of being vir-

Character Education in Theory 107

tuous in the first place—or at least, beginning to practice the virtues" (p. 95). Evidently, for Kilpatrick, reason, choice, and decision-making are all unimportant in moral education. Moral formation means acquiring virtues and continually practicing those virtues.

Thus, these influential writers promote character education as content centered and involving direct teaching of virtues. As we will see in the next chapter, the trait list and the direct instruction of virtues are indeed the benchmark of the character education programs in American schools. Such a model was a large part of the character education of the 1920s. Character educators, like Kilpatrick, realize this and urge us to return to that model, one that "took place in school and society in the past" (p. 16) and one that "seemed to serve our culture well over a long period of time" (p. 16). Kilpatrick praises the traditional character education philosophy that one cannot be a good person without any training in goodness and that children cannot learn to make good moral decisions without acquiring moral habits or strength of character.

Kilpatrick tirelessly reminds us how the traditional character education model functions: "There are traits of character children ought to know, that they learn these by example, and that once they know them, they need to practice them until they become second nature" (p. 15). Such a model of character education is markedly content centered. In the process of character education, teachers consciously

> teach specific virtues and character traits such as courage, justice, self-control, honesty, responsibility, charity, obedience to lawful authority, etc. These concepts are introduced and explained and then illustrated by memorable examples from history, literature, and current events. (p. 93)

The role of stories and role models in moral formation is thus greatly emphasized. Character educators use stories to transmit virtues and people of virtue as examples to model behaviors. Where are these virtues drawn from? They are richly embedded in traditional cultures, argues Kilpatrick: "Traditional cultures made generous use of epics, stories, songs, painting, and sculpture in educating and socializing the young. In many ways it was a surprisingly up-to-date approach—what we would now call 'teaching to the right brain'" (p. 24).

Kilpatrick also affirms the philosophical roots of character education. Under his direction, we can trace the origins of character education to ancient

Greek and Roman times, particularly to the virtue ethics of Aristotle. According to Kilpatrick, character education is based on a somewhat dim view of human nature (one largely compatible with character educators' embrace of the Judeo-Christian doctrine, as I shall discuss later). This view holds that good conduct does not come naturally. Thus,

> The chief way to counter our lack of will and determination is through the development of good habits. An effective moral education would be developed to encouraging habits of honesty, helpfulness, and self-control until such behaviors become second nature. (p. 97)

"This is how the ancient Greeks and Romans understood moral education," Kilpatrick claims. Setting aside Socrates' doubts on the possibility of teaching virtues, Kilpatrick and other character educators embrace Aristotle's endorsement of such teaching. Kilpatrick writes: "Aristotle said that a man becomes virtuous by performing virtuous acts; he becomes kind by doing kind acts; he becomes brave by doing brave acts" (p. 97). Thus, while embracing Aristotle's philosophy, Kilpatrick, and other character educators as well, defines character education as behavioral training. Children should be trained in morally appropriate modes of behavior as defined by authoritative adults. Children's personal needs and abilities in this area are ignored. Adult demands in the form of community/societal values become norms and rules, but individual rights are sacrificed. Aristotle and his modern followers all believe that children are not yet able to reason about moral issues. They need guidance, supervision, or, simply put, control. In Aristotle's eyes, the behavioral training of children was necessary in maintaining the rigid class structure of society. Is it not fair to say that Kilpatrick and other character educators are striving for that too?

Wynne: For Religion-Based Moral Education

We now move on to the ideas of another character education leader, Edward A. Wynne. Wynne was a professor of education at the University of Illinois at Chicago and an outspoken advocate for traditional character education. His call for character education goes further and is more specific than Bennett's and Kilpatrick's in that he argues for a total and thorough return to a traditional, content-centered, and even religion-based moral education.

Like Bennett and Kilpatrick, Wynne (1989a, 1989b) openly argues, without any hesitation, that schools must transmit traditional values to students. He declares that transmission of traditional central values is the core of any society and certainly the cure for declining modern American society. Where his idea of moral education differs is in his explicit definition of "traditional values" as "the panoply of virtues connoted by phrases such as the work ethic and obedience to legitimate authority and by the important nonreligious themes articulated in the Ten Commandments" (1989a, p. 19).

In another article, Wynne (1989b) addresses the moral nature of "effective schools," a major education movement in the 1980s. William Bennett, then Secretary of Education, also praised the effective-schools formula as utilizing strong leaders, emphasizing the basics, and teaching values. Wynne extols the traditional model of moral education in effective schools, listing a number of traditional moral values that he claims constitute the moral elements of the effective schools. His list includes (1) "the acceptance of traditional hierarchy" (p.129), (2) "the exercise of strong adult control over children and adolescents" (p.130), (3) "the priority given to immediate good conduct over more elaborate ratiocination"(p.130), (4) "great emphasis on the life of collective entities" (p.130), (5) "reverence for the knowledge of the past" (p.131), (6) "the reservation of a sphere of life for sacred activities, beyond the day-to-day business of buying, selling, and producing" (p.131), and (7) "the equality of all community members as children of God, despite their temporal, material, and intellectual differences" (p.132).

According to Wynne, the traditional moral values of the Judeo-Christian ethic have pervaded both private and public schools in the United States. He declares that effective schools are essentially traditional schools based on these values (p. 138). Wynne finds that these effective schools have produced students with "good character." The numerous signs of such good character vary but essentially embody the following qualities: good discipline, obedience to adult authority, strong academic commitment, heightened collective identity, and collective loyalty.

We see an exclusive and inappropriate version of character or morality in Wynne's account. Wynne and his supporters may argue that such a version of moral education is well grounded in tradition and culture, but their religion-based approach causes serious concerns in a culturally diverse society. One has good reason to wonder whether a public school will still remain a school for the public if it transforms itself according to Wynne's prescription. If we were to apply Wynne's character education scheme to schools, we would radically alter the nature and direction of public education in this country.

The overall traditional model of effective schools is seriously flawed. As Stedman (1987) argues, "The lack of research support for the formula raises serious questions about the programs that have been based on it" (p. 216); therefore, the widely cited set of characteristics of effective schools cannot be substantiated. Furthermore, Stedman found:

> In concentrating on the basics and testing, however, the current reform movement ignores the cultural nature of schooling. The typical school remains a white, middle-class institution whose language and worldview are alien to members of different cultures and classes. (pp. 218–219)

Stedman determined that truly effective schools emphasized cultural pluralism, drew on community resources, and involved parents and teachers in school governance. Stedman's findings directly counter the cultural bias in Wynne's arrogant claim that effective schools are rooted in traditional Judeo-Christian moral education.

Despite all of the criticism, Wynne (1989b) does believe that the Judeo-Christian-rooted values are or should be shared by all the people in America. He argues, "It is not surprising that persons reared in the United States, a country with a long tradition of Judeo-Christian commitment, should feel affiliation with such values, regardless of their personal religious commitments" (p. 129). Wynne simply does not accept possible rejections of the Judeo-Christian values by non-Judeo-Christian people in the country and dictates what he and his followers believe to be universal values.

Wynne's claim represents a major weakness in the character education movement. The movement advocates the teaching of universal values, but in actuality, it promotes the values of particular ideologies. The leaders of character education reject moral relativism; however, they present recommendations that seem to be relative themselves. They present the Judeo-Christian values as absolute, universal values; this is anything but the truth. We will revisit this very important issue later in this chapter.

Lickona and Ryan: Translating Theory into Practice

Bennett, Kilpatrick, and Wynne argue for direct teaching of virtues, the rigorous training of behaviors, and a total return to Western tradition. Their views largely define the philosophical and ideological nature of character education and set the direction for educational practices. Within this framework and direction, Thomas Lickona and Kevin Ryan's works on character education include more specific curricular and pedagogical ramifications. They attempt to combine their moral philosophy with practical concerns. Leaving their specific stances aside, they have done an exceptional job of translating theory into practice, more specifically, translating their moral philosophy into character education programming.

One major feature of the strategies developed by Lickona and Ryan is a "comprehensive approach" to character education, which makes their theory of character education seem different from that of Bennett (1993), Kilpatrick (1992), and Wynne (1989a, 1989b). The comprehensive approach is appealing to many character educators and is even acknowledged by some critics of the movement (Noddings, 1995). It has given some character educators a foundation for their argument. For example, responding to Alfie Kohn's (1997b) charge that current character education practice is dominated by a narrow vision of morality and moral education, Lickona (1998) argues that character educators "agree on the need for a broad approach," and the principle has been promoted by many character education centers and organizations. However, Lickona does not convince his critics that character educators in practice are indeed committed to the comprehensive principle (see chapter 5 for this argument), nor is he convincing in his argument that the comprehensive approach itself is really comprehensive in nature. As we will see, and as Kohn has correctly pointed out, the comprehensive approach represents one particular and narrow notion of morality and moral education and falls within the category prescribed by Bennett, Kilpatrick, and Wynne.

A "Comprehensive" Concept of Character

According to Lickona and Ryan, a comprehensive character education approach has, first of all, a comprehensive concept of character, and, second, a comprehensive approach to developing that character. Ryan (1989) articulates a comprehensive vision of the moral agent, contending that "human character arises from the workings of three components: knowing, affect, and action" (p. 7). Lickona (1991) obviously agrees with Ryan:

> Character so conceived has three interrelated parts: moral knowing, moral feeling, and moral behavior. *Good character consists of knowing the good, desiring the good, and doing the good*—habits of the mind, habits of the heart, and habits of the action. All three are necessary for leading a moral life; all three make up moral maturity. (p. 51)

Lickona repeats the same message in a widely cited 1993 article in *Educational Leadership* in which he emphasizes that "character must be broadly conceived to encompass the cognitive, affective, and behavioral aspects of morality. Good character consists of knowing the good, desiring the good, and doing the good" (p. 9).

Unlike Bennett and Kilpatrick, who place most emphasis on the behavioral aspect, Lickona and Ryan seem to stress all three aspects. This should be viewed as progress in the theoretical development of character education. Lickona and Ryan acknowledge the cognitive side of character and admit that it is required for full moral maturity. Lickona even includes specific qualities such as perspective-taking, moral reasoning, and decision-making in the cognitive dimension, which are highly emphasized by Kohlberg's model and almost totally excluded from the model developed by Bennett, Kilpatrick, and Wynne.

However, Lickona makes it clear that his emphasis is still on the behavioral aspect of character, stressing a need for the predictable and desirable behavior in children. He notes that no one can guarantee that a moral person will automatically act morally: "There are times...when we may know what we should do, feel we should do it, but still fail to translate thought and feeling into action" (Lickona, 1991, p. 61). Therefore, the behavioral aspect must be stressed, moving a person to act morally and keeping him/her doing so by working on the three aspects of character: competence, will, and habit (61). In a later article, Lickona (1998) admits his bias: "Character education is distinctive in its emphasis on promoting moral behavior, on giving students repeated opportunities to practice good behavior until it becomes a matter of habit—a virtue" (p. 454).

Despite their emphasis on the integration of different aspects of morality, both Ryan and Lickona still share with Bennett, Kilpatrick, and Wynne the most important assumption: Moral education is content based and virtue cen-

Character Education in Theory

tered. For example, right after proposing his broad concept of character, Lickona (1993) states: "Schools must help children understand the core values, adopt or commit to them, and then act upon them in their own lives" (p. 9). This statement clearly indicates that Lickona, like Bennett, believes that the existence of core values is objective, to have a good character is to possess these values, and the purpose of character education is the development of these values via the cognitive, affective, and behavioral channels. The ultimate goal is unquestionably virtue. The crucial steps are development of the virtue, internalization of the virtue, and manifestation of the virtue, and all these require various efforts from one's mind, heart, and will. This view fundamentally differs from other moral education theories that emphasize the contextual nature of morality and doubt that it is possible to teach values directly.

Ryan's (1989) articulation of the cognitive component of the moral agent actually mirrors what Bennett and Kilpatrick argue about and downplays his own occasional emphasis on moral reasoning. He realizes that man is a being with the ability to reason, existing within a community. Then he claims that there are "certain patterns of behavior and certain human character traits and virtues necessary to sustain the life of the individual and the community" (p. 7). Man must master these traits or virtues. One cannot debate about whether those traits or virtues exist or how they exist or whether they deserve to be pursued. One just needs to acknowledge them. One needs to know what these virtues are, what they require of man in concrete cases, and what the consequences are if one does not have these virtues. This is very similar to what Bennett notes in his *The Book of Virtues*: "The purpose of this book is to show parents, teachers, students, and children what the virtues look like, what they are in practice, how to recognize them, and how they work" (p. 11).

Thus, the so-called comprehensive concept of character is exclusively defined in terms of the cultivation of virtues and the direct training of behaviors. Lickona (1991) states: "Character consists of *operative values*, values in action. We progress in our character as a value becomes a virtue, a reliable inner disposition to respond to situations in a morally good way" (p. 51). And in a 1999 article, Lickona reaffirms his definition of character and character education:

> Character education is the deliberate effort to cultivate virtue. Virtues are objectively good human qualities, such as a commitment to truth, wisdom, honesty, compassion, courage, diligence, perseverance, and self-control. Virtues are good for the

individual in that they are required to lead a fulfilling life. They are good for the human community in that they enable us to live together harmoniously and productively. Virtues are grounded in human nature and experience; they provide a standard for defining good character. (p. 23)

Such a definition suggests that Lickona and Ryan's idea of character education only slightly differs from that of Bennett, Kilpatrick, and Wynne.

Like Bennett and Kilpatrick, Lickona and Ryan argue for the teaching of moral literacy, which helps locate the virtues sought by character educators. According to Ryan (1989), moral literacy is best represented by "the best literature" and "the best history," where "the moral lessons…are embedded" (p. 8). He also states: "The emphasis on the moral agent's knowing means that students need to come to know their culture's moral wisdom, that is what has been learned over the years" (p. 7). This is the most important goal of character education, argues Ryan. "Character development puts a heavy emphasis on culture…it places more emphasis on the traditional role of the school as transmitter of the culture" (p. 14). Thus, we see a necessary connection between Ryan's claim and Wynne's. As Ryan himself admits: "The vital and primary energies of the teachers and students should be centered around knowing what Edward Wynne (1985/86) calls the 'Great Tradition.'…Cultural literacy and the traditional content of school are of central importance in character development" (p. 15).

A "Comprehensive" Approach to Character Development

Thus far, the general concept of character and character education as defined by Lickona and Ryan has been introduced. Now let us look at what their "comprehensive approach" requires for instruction. Lickona (1999) describes the central components of such an approach in this way:

> To be effective, character education must be comprehensive, intentionally making use of every phase of school life as an opportunity to develop good character. A comprehensive approach seeks to foster virtue through the teacher's example, the subject matter of the curriculum, the rigor of the academic standards, the conduct of sports and other extracurricular activities, the handling of rules and discipline, and the school's intellectual and moral climate. A comprehensive approach recognizes that everything in a school's moral life affects character, for good or for ill. (p. 23)

Lickona first developed this approach in his 1991 book and later modified and emphasized it in many articles (Lickona, 1993, 1996, 1997, 1999). His comprehensive approach includes "nine character-building strategies for the classroom" and "three schoolwide strategies."[1] In these strategies, Lickona addresses all forces in and out of schools that affect students' character. He insists that all faculty members are moral educators. He sees all areas of the school environment as part of a moral community, specifying discipline, academic curriculum, and extracurricular activities as avenues of character education. He argues for a school-home-community partnership for building character. These strategies are promoted as a road map to develop the three aspects of character, which are centered around virtues. They have been widely advertised and distributed through his writings and presentations at his annual summer institutes.

As Lickona (1998) informs us, many character education organizations agree on the need for this broad approach. For example, the Character Education Partnership (CEP), the nation's leading character education organization with a sizable membership, has been working to implement such a comprehensive approach. In 1995, the CEP published *Eleven Principles of Effective Character Education,* by Thomas Lickona, Eric Schaps, and Catherine Lewis, which offers schools a set of standards by which they can plan and assess a character education initiative.[2] The eleven principles promote a virtue-centered, comprehensive character education approach and are very similar to Lickona's nine-plus-three character education strategies.

Further Inquiry into Character Education Theory

The rest of this chapter extends the inquiry into the common ground of the philosophical and ideological orientations of the character education theories. In particular, it focuses on three highly notable yet problematic features of character education theory: the "holistic" view of education, the virtue-centered moral training approach, and the religious connotations of character education proposals.

A "Holistic" View of Education and the Moralism That Lies Within

As was illustrated in the previous chapter, character education leaders claim that moral decay is responsible for social ills and that moral education is crucial for countering social problems. In addition, the leaders sometimes justify character education from another standpoint, claiming that the teaching of ethics and values is an integral purpose of schools and that character education is central to the education of a whole child.

Such a perspective reflects a holistic view which has always been promoted in the history of education. In the 1920s, the National Education Association, an organization that played an influential role in the promotion of character education, declared that "the ultimate objective of popular education is to teach the children how to live righteously, healthily, and happily.... The building of character is the real aim of schools" (in Yulish, 1980, p. 28). Embedded within this declaration is the idea that academic training—reading, writing, and arithmetic—is just one part of the preparation for the ultimate object, human well-being. Today, character educators express the same concern. Lickona (1991) adds respect and responsibility as the fourth and fifth Rs to be included in the school curriculum because he believes moral values are integral elements. As we will see in the next chapter, many National Schools of Character do not overtly address the issue of moral decline in the society (although I believe it is still one of their rationales); rather, they emphasize moral teaching as a task they are obligated to perform.

Character educators are not alone in advocating a holistic view of education. Theorists and educators, from John Dewey to Nel Noddings, have supported holistic education. Dewey spoke explicitly against the traditional model of character education but regarded the separation of the intellectual and the moral as lamentable. In her many works on modern school reform, Noddings voices her strong opposition to academic training as the sole purpose of schooling and urges schools to embrace the nonacademic aspects of the child's life as well. As she states, the aim of schools "should be to encourage the growth of competent, caring, loving, and lovable people" (Noddings, 1992, p. xiv).

Character educators welcome these statements in their belief that educators like Dewey and Noddings generally agree with them on the moral mission of schools. These educators may agree with them on other points. For example, in her latest book on moral education, *Educating Moral People: A Caring Alternative to Character Education,* Noddings (2002) acknowledges the efforts of character educators to use examples and stories. Despite these areas of agreement, however, both Dewey and Noddings, along with other progressive educators, are still important critics of the character education approach. For example, both Dewey (1897/1974, 1909, 1934) and Noddings (2002) criticize the core of character education—the virtue-centered approach to moral training—and instead promote progressive and construction-

Character Education in Theory

ist views of morality and moral education. Character educators do not bother to clarify the fundamental differences between their theories and those of educators like Dewey and Noddings but focus instead on the similarities.

We must critically look at character educators' holistic view of education and ask whether this view would actually promote the education of the whole child. A truly holistic perspective recognizes and appreciates all of the child's developmental needs and strengths and stresses educational efforts to address these needs and accentuate those strengths. A holistic perspective also points out flaws and suggests reforms. For example, Noddings's holistic perspective and theory of moral education are based on her criticism of the fundamental school structure and culture that prevent the child's development into a well-rounded person. In particular, she targets the current efforts that promote tougher academic standards and excessive testing. She argues that such moves do not adequately meet the developmental and educational needs of today's students. Teaching more mathematics and physics does not ensure a happy life for any student; preparing everyone for college is not the sole purpose of schooling. Her moral education approach reorganizes the school around centers of care and encourages "the growth of competent, caring, loving, and lovable people" (Noddings, 1992, p. xiv), people considered to be truly well rounded.

Character educators do not address the fundamental problems of schools in their claims for holistic education and character education. They recognize that a total absence of moral education is not in the best interests of the students, but they fail to realize that current practices such as additional stress and a myopic focus on standards and tests prevent genuine moral education.

The leaders of character education strongly support the current standards-driven educational policies. Bennett (1992) talks about three Cs: content, character, and choice. He argues for a more rigorous common (standardized) curriculum and believes that moral training will buttress the installation of just such a curriculum. Wynne and Ryan (1997) promote the connection of character, academics, and discipline. They emphasize that "moral instruction is fully consistent with students attaining excellent academic results" (p. vii). As for Lickona (1991, 1998), he makes specific recommendations as to how educators can teach virtues, such as responsibility and respect, in terms of the school's academic standards. He claims that the improvement in students' scoring on standardized tests is one of the "positive effects" of character education in schools (Lickona, 1998).

Obviously, character education leaders do not challenge the overall school structure and educational policies that hinder the actualization of holistic education. A character education scheme that supports and reinforces harmful educational practices such as standardized testing can hardly promote the child's moral development. Therefore, it is doubtful that character educators are truly advocating a holistic educational philosophy.

Another potential problem that could arise from the so-called holistic education is that character education leaders may emphasize the moral aspect of schooling and, moreover, may embrace moralism. Taking a stand for a well-rounded education has already become a strategy for Chinese authorities who want to impose communist-controlled moral education on all students. The promise of holistic education turns out to be a perfect excuse for maintaining politicized moral education in schools. Moralistic schooling sets up standards, rules, and duties in support of the dominant political ideologies and controls the personal needs, inclinations, and affections of students. We must remain critical about the similar claims of holistic education and moral teaching in the character education movement in the United States. Character educators remind us of the importance of educating for the well-being of the whole child, which is indeed an ideal all educators ought to pursue. However, their approach tends to reduce the complexity of ethics to a code of moral minutiae. We must express doubt about such a moralistic tendency.

Virtue-Centered Moral Education
Character education has always been overwhelmingly virtue centered. Early character educators, like White (1909) and McKown (1935), developed the basic framework of character education: The general elements that make up the attractive character are traits or virtues; therefore, the purpose of character education is the development of these traits or virtues. As discussed in chapter 2, the development of character traits or moral virtues was a central goal of character education practices as long ago as the 1920s and 1930s.

Modern character educators continue this tradition without reservation. Advocates usually define character as the possession and manifestation of virtues and character education as the cultivation of virtues. Theorists, especially Kilpatrick and Wynne, repeatedly remind us of the importance and effectiveness of the traditional traits-centered character education approach and urge a return to it.

As noted when we discussed Aristotle's virtue ethics, the direct teaching of virtues inevitably turns out to be behavioral training that ignores individual rights and moral reasoning. Behavioral training always establishes political and social control. Other issues must be tackled as well. The definition of character as the possession of virtues is problematic. Such a definition implies that character is fixed and a person of good character possesses certain fixed virtues. This is a simplistic and apathetic view of character, which is actually dynamic and interactive. As Dewey (1897/1974) argues, character is "a piece of running, physical machinery" (p. 133). Character cannot be conceived simply in terms of results. Character, as a power of agency, has multiple constituents such as force, judgment, and emotional responsiveness. It constantly develops within a social web, involving constructive reactions to life's varied contingencies and active moral inquiry and imagination. It has ethical flexibility and involves the ability to make moral decisions. Such a progressive and constructionist perspective of character is also supported by Robert Coles (1986), who claims that character is "no rigid, categorical trait...character is not a possession, but something one searches for: a quality of mind and heart one struggles for" (pp. 143–144).

Character educators' non-contextual definition of universal virtues as objective and absolute existences is more troubling. Lickona (1999) states that "virtues are objectively good human qualities....Virtues are grounded in human nature and experience. They provide a standard for defining good character" (p. 23). Because virtues are presumably objective, character educators assume that a consensus on the virtues to be transmitted can be reached. Thus, the so-called universality of virtues is a popular concept in the movement. Character education leaders create lists of so-called universal or common values to be taught (Bennett, 1993; Lickona, 1991). Values on the lists include respect, responsibility, honesty, fairness, caring, courage, self-discipline, compassion, etc. As we will see in chapter 5, character education schools respond to the call of their leaders as they create their lists of universal values and organize all the educational activities around these lists.

This view of virtues as objective existences reflects certain aspects of moral absolutism. Character educators designate certain meanings to a group of values and claim that people of different backgrounds share them. They ignore the situations or contexts of values, which may well cause people to have different interpretations of such values. Progressive educators strongly criticize absolutism and argue that virtues (or values) may be involved in good character, but they are not fixed and absolute but context dependent. Any ethical behavior is related to a particular situation. For example, Dewey (1909) denied the assumption of moral principles as "arbitrary" (p. 58) and "transcendental" (p. 58). He also argued:

> We believe in moral laws and rules, to be sure, but they are in the air. They are something set off by themselves. They are so very "moral" that there is no working contact between them and the average affairs of everyday life. What we need is to have these moral principles brought down to the ground through their statement in social and psychological terms. (1897/1974, p. 137)

In agreement with Dewey, Hartshorne and May (1928–1930) pointed out that morality is basically a function of the situations in which the moral subject (the person) is placed. Noddings (1995) also argues for the situational and contextual nature of morality. Her analysis reveals that virtues like courage and honesty are always socially constructed.

It is not difficult for us to reflect upon our personal experiences and then agree upon the arguments provided by the progressive educators. There are always different demonstrations of forms or manifestations of morality across various cultures. The interpretations of a specific moral quality may also change according to different situations even within one culture. For example, in American culture (let us take "American culture" as one culture although it is actually diverse), honesty is as highly regarded as it is in Chinese culture. However, unlike American doctors, few doctors in China would be completely honest and tell a cancer patient that he/she has cancer. (In China cancer is still widely viewed as incurable. Chinese doctors do not tell patients that they are going to die, but Americans do.) Thus, the essence of honesty does not exist independently of certain social and cultural contexts. The term "honesty" means different things to different people depending on the circumstances.

Take courage as another example. During the Cultural Revolution in China, young people were allowed to destroy various representations of the ancient cultural tradition such as the religious sites and artistic works of the country. Their behavior was widely acclaimed as courageous then, but today we genuinely mourn the great loss of Chinese culture and condemn those acts as destructive and those responsible as criminals. More recently, in the Middle East conflict, suicide bombing has become a new form of violence. You may call it terrorism—from the Israeli perspective—or a new form of

Character Education in Theory 121

resistance—in the eyes of Palestinians—nevertheless, the act itself, sacrificing one's own life for a great cause, is courageous. However, it is probably difficult for most people in the world to applaud this particular courageous act.

We may come to terms with virtues like these on a daily basis. We may encounter circumstances within which we must make moral decisions that may require us to reflect upon the meanings of certain virtues. However, virtues alone are unlikely to make us either virtuous or non-virtuous. One is unlikely to be either bad or good in most life situations. Ambiguity and uncertainty are norms of life. We always "live" virtues in our own ways. Honesty is mentioned over and over again, yet, who can tell us what honesty exactly means for everyone? As Coles (1986) asks: "Who is 'really' honest, and for what 'underlying' reasons? Moreover, does it 'pay' in this society to be honest all the time? When do honesty and self-effacement turn into 'masochism'? When does pride in one's convictions turn into bullying egotism?" (p. 142). Can telling children to be honest without addressing these questions really make them honest persons?

Tolerance and respect are also listed as absolute, universal values. But my understanding of tolerance may differ from yours. Many questions could be asked: What is tolerance for? For diversity? What kind of diversity? Should all life styles be tolerated? Should marijuana use be tolerated as alcohol use is? Should all beliefs be tolerated? If religious beliefs are to be tolerated, what about the fundamentalist Christian belief that homosexuality is a sin? Will we get the same answers to these questions from different people?

What does respect mean? For many people, teaching respect means teaching children to respect adults and other forms of authority. But why do children have to respect adults and authority? What is the rationale? What if the authority does not deserve respect at all? Respect for authority could quickly end up becoming blind obedience to authority. Is this what all people mean by respect?

These and many other examples tell us that although we do share a general endorsement of many moral values, we may only share the metaphysical forms of the values such as "honesty" or "respect" or "tolerance." In other words, a virtue may appear to be universal and timeless, but its actual content—its application in practice—is always particular and relative to the circumstance in question. We may differ fundamentally in what these virtues actually mean for us in different situations. Such understanding of the non-absolute and nonuniversal nature of morality may, as Noddings (1995) notes, leave us "feeling a bit rudderless at sea, but this suggests the need for a careful analysis of the virtues described in character education programs and a dialogue on how various groups interpret them" (p. 151).

While character educators believe that their views reflect absolute truths, in actuality, they are proponents of particular moral ideologies and, therefore, make relative recommendations. As we have seen, Wynne's (1989a, 1989b) praise for traditional moral values stems exclusively from his preference for the Judeo-Christian tradition. His definition of so-called common virtues is explicitly based on his religious beliefs. Lickona (1991) stresses the teacher's responsibility to keep students working up to the standards, but, as Noddings (2002) asks, "Why should the assignment and correction of homework be listed as demands of teacher responsibility? Why should a teacher's insistence that all students meet a uniform standard be a sign of either respect or caring?" (p. 10). These examples show us how a given writer or a teacher would arrive at his own interpretation of a particular virtue. The views of morality or character are entirely based upon personal beliefs or ideologies. So, although character educators' recommendations of common virtues are supposedly derived from absolute moral principles, they seem strikingly relative at their core. The claim of universality is used to conceal the relative nature of their claims. Character educators do not promote moral relativism because moral relativism holds that anyone's values are valid; they assume their own values as absolute, superior to others' values.

In addition, while emphasizing a list of certain values as common values, character educators implicitly downplay the pluralism of values. By prescribing a specific list of virtues which is by no means all-inclusive, character educators overlook many other values which are significant to the lives of people. For example, as Noddings (2002) argues, character educators overwhelmingly emphasize "standard moral values" in their programs but neglect personality traits, intellectual virtues, and physical qualities which are important for a good life.

Moreover, character educators' moral values are mostly rooted in Western tradition as Bennett and Wynne explicitly and repetitively argued. Since Western tradition certainly does not represent the entire world, the claim of universality is seriously undermined, exposed as a deceptive perception without any possibility of realization.

The problems of virtue-centeredness will be further discussed later when we examine the practice of character education. Now let us move on to an-

Character Education in Theory

other significant theoretical aspect of character education—religious influences.

Religious Influences

A connection between religion and character education is a goal for the leaders of character education. In *The Book of Virtues*, Bennett (1993) emphasizes faith as the ultimate virtue to be instilled in children. He claims:

> A human being without faith, without *reverence* for anything, is a human being morally adrift. The world's major religions provide time-tested anchors for drifters....Faith can contribute important elements to the social stability and moral development of individuals and groups. (pp. 741–742)

In their 1996 book, Bennett, Dilulio, and Walters believe that the religious dimension of moral poverty is the most important dimension of all. In addressing moral poverty, they argue, "The most obvious answer—and perhaps the only reliable answer—is a widespread renewal of religious faith and the strengthening of religious institutions" (p. 208). Lickona agrees with Bennett and urges us to recognize the role of religion in moral education. Lickona (1999) makes two points: Religion contributes to civic virtue, and religion can protect young people against high-risk and antisocial behavior. He argues that without religion's call to the transcendent, most people would be more tempted to abuse human capacities and be conquered by worldly evils. The condition of our democracy has been affected by religion, argues Lickona. He cites a report of the Council on Civil Society and claims that a central task of every generation is transmission of morality: "Religion historically has probably been the primary force that transmits from one generation to another the moral understandings that are essential to liberal democratic institutions" (Lickona, 1999, p. 22). His argument that religion protects youth against high-risk and antisocial behavior is based on a single study by two other researchers. Lickona agrees with their claim that religion helps to prevent teenagers from turning to illegal drugs, sexual involvement, and delinquency.

Then Lickona (1999) goes one step further and suggests seven ways to incorporate religion into character education.[3] He urges schools to teach students to recognize and appreciate religion's role in the formation of American democracy and religious motivation in the lives of individuals. He advises schools to construct specific curricula that include religion and to encourage students to use faith traditions to deal with social and life issues. He especially urges schools to draw upon religion as a support for abstinence-based sex education. He also emphasizes that schools should draw upon religion to teach students objective and absolute moral truths and engage those truths in addressing life's ultimate questions.

Edward Wynne (1989a, 1989b) also connects religion and character education. He might be the one who takes this matter to the farthest extreme. He openly and straightforwardly argues for the direct teaching of Judeo-Christian moral values. For him, religion, specifically, Judaism and Christianity, is not only a reference moral educators can make and relate to when teaching moral values but also the final and fundamental source for moral education. So there is a general consensus among these leaders that religion is crucial in character education, and schools must systematically use religion for the purpose of moral development and character building.

We must dialectically examine the role of religion in our history, culture, and human life in general and moral life in particular. Unfortunately, such dialectical thinking is missing from these leaders' overall endorsement of religion. While recognizing and appreciating the positive role religion has played on all fronts, they largely ignore the fact that religion, especially institutionalized religion, has also been an oppressive force in human history. It is true that "faith is a source of discipline and power and meaning in the lives of the faithful of any major religious creed. It is a potent force in human experience" (Bennett, 1993, p. 742). But what this force can bring to human lives is an open question. Many may answer this question in a way that reveals the very dark side of religion.

For example, as Bennett himself recognizes, while a shared faith binds people together, clashing faiths divide people, sometimes in violent ways. History has repeatedly demonstrated how a group of people bound by a given religious faith can commit terrible crimes against other people, even the deviant members within their own group. Think about the Crusades, the Inquisition, and the religious fever behind the most recent human tragedies in the Middle East and the United States. One must be wary of the generalization that religion is necessarily connected to human goodness. Religion does not always represent and promote humanity in general and morality in particular.

Some of Lickona's assertions deserve further discussion. He is right when he says "the exclusion of religion from the public school curriculum is neither intellectually honest nor in the public interest" (Lickona, 1999, p. 23).

Religion has indeed been largely and inappropriately marginalized in public schools, and it should be restored to its *rightful* place in the study of history, culture, and morality. But we do not need a total restoration of religious indoctrination in school curricula and religious dominance in moral education as Lickona's proposals imply.

Once again, we acknowledge that religions have been important sources of morality and have provided considerable justification for morality. In fact, moral education in the United States was unquestionably related to certain religious traditions throughout most of its history. Today, for countless people, religion still elevates, dignifies, ritualizes, and defines human experiences and plays a motivating and even determining role in their moral lives. However, such recognition does not necessarily justify a total return of religion to today's moral education for all children. Respect for constitutional separation of church and state and commitment to cultural diversity make us critical of such an absolute return.

Today, we need to teach *about* religions, and teach about them *critically*. James Giarelli (1993) praises Noddings' book, *Educating for Intelligent Belief or Unbelief,* asserting that we need to "make questions of religious belief and unbelief a subject of inquiry, connected to the other qualities and moods of our humanness" (in Noddings, 1993, p. ix). Under this guideline, including religion in moral education in public schools requires us to both appreciate and critique religion's role in defining morality; to use religion as a reference, not an ultimate and dominant source; to engage students in moral reflection; and to encourage students to inquire and explore the ultimate, the sacred, and the existential meanings and purposes of education, moral education, and life.

Bringing religion back to moral education, under character education leaders' schemes, means to uncritically embrace religious dominance in moral life, to utilize the conservative force of religion in training students' behaviors, and to indoctrinate and normalize students to dominant religious influences and their associated social and political discourses. These proposals are not in the best interest of public schools. In addition, although religion may be crucial to many people's moral development and character building, it may not be crucial to all. In some cases, it may be used to create a homogeneous vision of America. Character education leaders' recommendations imply the imposition of certain religions on all students. This is not only unconstitutional but also morally problematic.

Many have critically examined the religion-based character education proposals and revealed their ideological underpinnings. Singer (1994), for example, points out that although parents and religious leaders have the right to teach teenagers the religious values that they consider important, no one has the right "to use the public schools to impose their personal religious beliefs on their teenagers and on other people's teenage children" (p. 78). Bennetta (1994) argues that Lickona's abstinence-based sex education reflects the ideologies of the Religious Right. He examines the connection between Lickona's views and some notorious political outlets such as Teen-Aid and Sex Respect. These agencies had been financially supported by the Reagan and Bush administrations and had consistently promoted conservative forces against abortion and homosexuality.

Character education leaders are trying their best to connect character education and religion. Actually, as some critics point out, such a connection is already a reality. Alfie Kohn's (1997a, 1997b) examination of character education led him to conclude that values emphasized by the leaders and the practitioners, such as hard work, obedience, hierarchy, respect for authority, sexual restraint, etc., are distinctly conservative and are reflections of Protestant ethics. Similarly, David Purpel (1999) finds that

> the values taught in the schools are very much in the line of Puritan traditions of obedience, hierarchy, and hard work, values which overlap nicely with the requirements of an economic system that values a compliant and industrious work force, and a social system that demands stability and order. (p. 89)

As Kohn and Purpel illustrate, religion is intrinsically linked to the character education movement. Not only is religion promoted by the movement, in turn, the movement is influenced and shaped by religion.

Notes

1. The nine classroom strategies Lickona proposes are:
    (1) The teacher as caregiver, model, and ethical mentor: treating students with love and respect, encouraging right behavior, and correcting wrongful actions.
    (2) A caring classroom community: teaching students to respect and care about each other.
    (3) Moral discipline: using rules and consequences to develop moral reasoning, self-control, and a generalized respect for others.

Character Education in Theory 127

   (4) A democratic classroom environment: using the class meeting to engage students in shared decision making and in taking responsibility for making the classroom the best it can be.
   (5) Teaching values through the curriculum: using the ethically rich content of academic subjects as vehicles for values teaching.
   (6) Cooperative learning: fostering students' ability to work with and appreciate others.
   (7) The "conscience of craft": developing students' sense of academic responsibility and the habit of doing their work well.
   (8) Ethical reflection: developing the cognitive side of character through reading, research, writing, and discussion.
   (9) Conflict resolution: teaching students how to solve conflicts fairly, without intimidation or violence.

   The three strategies for the whole school include:
   (1) Caring beyond the classroom: using role models to inspire the altruistic behavior and providing opportunities for school and community service.
   (2) Creating a positive moral culture in the school: developing a caring school community that promotes the core values.
   (3) Parents and the community as partners: Helping parents and the whole community join the schools in a cooperative effort to build good character.

2. CEP's eleven principles of effective character education include:
   (1) Character education promotes core ethical values as the basis of good character.
   (2) Character must be comprehensively defined to include thinking, feeling, and behavior.
   (3) Effective character education requires an intentional, proactive, and comprehensive approach that promotes the core values in all phases of school life.
   (4) The school must be a caring community.
   (5) To develop character, students need opportunities for moral action.
   (6) Effective character education includes a meaningful and challenging academic curriculum that respects all learners and helps them succeed.
   (7) Character education should strive to develop students' intrinsic motivation.
   (8) The school staff must become a learning and moral community in which they share responsibility for character education and attempt to adhere to the same core values that guide the education of students.
   (9) Character education requires moral leadership from both staff and students.
   (10) The school must recruit parents and community members as full partners in the character-building effort.
   (11) Evaluation of character education should assess the character of the school; how the school staff members function as character educators, and the extent to which students manifest good character.

3. (1) Schools can help students understand the role religion has played in our moral beginnings as a nation.
   (2) Schools can teach that our country's major social reform movements—from the abolition of slavery to the civil rights movement—have been inspired by a religious

vision that life is sacred, that we are all equal in the sight of God, and that we are children of a common creator who calls us to live in harmony and justice.

(3) We can help students understand the role of religious motivation in the lives of individuals, both in history and in current times.

(4) Schools can select or construct specific curricula so as to include religion.

(5) Schools can encourage students to make use of all their intellectual and cultural resources, including their faith traditions, when they consider social issues (e.g., our obligation to the poor) and make personal moral decisions (e.g., whether to have sex before marriage).

(6) Schools can also draw upon religion as a way to engage students in considering the question, Is there moral truth?

(7) Schools can challenge students to develop a vision of life that addresses ultimate questions.

CHAPTER FIVE

Character Education in Practice: Linkages to Ideologies

Having examined the theoretical construction of character education and the ideological perspectives of its leading proponents, let us explore how the practice of character education connects to those fundamental ideologies. Although detailed case studies of particular character education programs are beyond the scope of this investigation, it is important to examine the practice at the macro level. This chapter will, therefore, draw upon the major reviews of exemplary character education programs to highlight the common themes of character education in practice.

It is not easy, however, to generalize about current character education programs. Like any other educational movement, this movement has multiple facets and defies simple characterization (Noddings, 1995; Leming, 1997). In the past decade, the number and variety of character education curricula have dramatically increased. Many individual schools have developed their own programs, which may lack clear philosophical and theoretical orientations. All "character education" programs may not necessarily share common ground. As Kohn (1997a) points out, the term "character education" now has multiple meanings: "In the broad sense, it refers to almost anything that schools might try to provide outside of academics, particularly when the purpose is to help children grow into good people" (p. 154). Schools across the country make many curricular efforts to address moral teaching, values instruction, or character building. They may identify these efforts as character education; however, their practice may not fall within the theoretical and pedagogical framework prescribed by leaders of character education such as William Bennett and Thomas Lickona.

As I noted in chapter 2, this study focuses on character education as a particular type of moral training advocated by Bennett, Kilpatrick, Wynne, Ryan, and Lickona, among others. The practice of character education of this kind has been supported by organizations such as The Character Education

Partnership (CEP) and The Center for the 4th and 5th Rs. This type of theory and practice represents the core of the current character education movement. Specific programs may vary, but it is still possible to generalize about their common features.

In the following pages, I will examine James Leming's influential review of ten contemporary programs that are considered excellent examples of the implementation of character education. In addition, the 2000 National Schools of Character, an award program sponsored by CEP, will be analyzed. These model schools have been selected to show other schools how to create a comprehensive approach to character building. Through these analytical efforts, I plan to illustrate and examine the common patterns across the exemplary programs, particularly their links to the ideological orientations advocated by the leaders of the movement.

Representative Character Education Programs

One of the best sources of information about contemporary character education programs is James Leming, one of the leading researchers in the field of moral education. He has reviewed various moral education programs in U.S. history, from the Kohlbergian programs to character education curricula. In his 1997 article, he reviewed ten "representative" contemporary character education programs. Leming set out to identify similarities and differences among these programs with regard to their objectives, pedagogy, and research. In so doing, he offered observations about the field of character education as a whole.

The ten programs were all produced by organizations or educational publishers.[1] According to Leming, these curricula were selected primarily on the basis of two criteria—self-identification as a character education program and presentation of their curricula at the annual meeting of either the CEP's annual Character Education Forum or the National Conference on Character Education, the two major character education conferences.

Leming (1997) found that all programs focus on the teaching of specific values or character traits and that all curricula are organized around these values or traits, which he refers to as character education objectives. He found that the language used to describe the objectives varies from program to program, for example, "values," "ethical principles," "character traits," "attributes of character," and "social skills."

In defining and describing these objectives, Leming (1997) noted, all the programs share one thing: "A claim of universality consistently accompanies the items that make up these lists of character education objectives. That is, the outcomes are presented as universal, common, core, or fundamental" (p. 26). There are obvious differences of opinion among curriculum developers as to the specific lists of values or traits. Some (such as responsibility, respect, and caring) show up on most lists, while others (such as hope, honor, family, and excellence) only show up on some lists. Nevertheless, all program developers claim to have a list of universal human values.

For example, the AEGIS program focuses on "six fundamental and universal ethical standards" including worth and dignity, rights and responsibility, fairness and justice, effort and excellence, care and consideration, and personal integrity and social responsibility (Leming, 1997, p. 16). The Character Education Curriculum teaches "12 universal values to children: honor, courage, conviction, honesty, truthfulness, generosity, kindness, helpfulness, justice, respect, freedom, and equality" (Leming, 1997, p. 17). The Child Development Project focuses on "four core values: fairness, concern and respect for others, helpfulness, and responsibility" (Leming, 1997, p. 18). The Heartwood Curriculum is organized around "seven character attributes that are universally accepted," which include courage, loyalty, justice, respect, hope, honesty, and love (Leming, 1997, p. 21).

One may wonder, since people do not agree upon what the "universal values" include, where does the so-called "universality" come from? Leming (1997) provided the following explanation: "Each curriculum has selected, for pedagogical purposes, a shorter list from a longer and more extensive list of truly universal values" (p. 26). For these character educators, and Leming as well, universal values indeed exist, and there are many to choose from. Each program can only focus on some, but certain values (such as respect, responsibility, and caring) are found on almost all the lists.

So, despite the disagreement as to which universal values are most important, program developers agree that good character means possessing and manifesting the so-called universal values. As Leming (1997) observed, "Underlying each curriculum's list of outcomes is the assumption that good character consists of an individual manifesting these outcomes in their behavior" (p. 27).

In terms of pedagogical orientation, Leming argues that most of the programs do not have a clear and explicit pedagogical understanding of how values are learned. The pedagogy is largely experience based. As he pointed out: "Rather than build an approach to character education from the psychological literature on character development or moralization, many of the developers of contemporary character education curricula have relied heavily on general teaching ideas and strategies derived from experienced teachers" (Leming, 1997, p. 29).

But Leming (1997) found a general pedagogical model shared by at least half of the reviewed curricula:

> This model consists of four steps. First, the students are exposed to a behavioral example of character education objective (virtue) that serves as the focus of the lesson. Typically students read or listen to a passage that contains a story or example of the desired character trait. Second, the students, through classroom discussion, attempt to explore meaning and to relate the character education objective to their personal experience or prior learning. Third, students apply their insights in a writing activity, or in a group activity such as role playing. Finally, students are encouraged to take some action in their own lives that will exemplify the character education objective. This model is typically implemented within a classroom and school climate consistent with the character education objectives of the curriculum, is interdisciplinary, and involves parents and the community as partners. (pp. 29–30)

This model largely reflects the comprehensive approach promoted by Lickona (1991) and would be endorsed by Bennett (1993) and other leaders of character education as well. The model certainly mirrors certain educational or curricular orientations.

Leming (1997) went on to discuss the "curricular orientations" of the character education programs, pointing out two major curricular orientations: cultural transmission and individual development. These two orientations have had a lasting and influential influence on curriculum development and educational practice in the United States. According to Leming, the cultural transmission orientation is rooted squarely in the classical academic tradition of Western culture and education, and, more recently, in behavioral psychology. From this perspective, knowledge and values are objective truths that are derived from the time-honored tradition of civilized life. As such, they are external and must be internalized by children and youth through imitation or explicit instruction accompanied by reward and punishment.

The individual development orientation holds, on the contrary, that the goal of education is the full development of individual potentialities. Development is interpreted as the result of the interaction between the child's innate capabilities and his environment.

Character Education in Practice

Leming found that both curricular orientations have been highly influential in shaping current character education programs. Three of the programs (AEGIS, Lessons in Character, and Lions-Quest), as a matter of relative emphasis, appear to draw more from the cultural transmission orientation. These programs

> place an emphasis on drawing students' attention to real or vicarious examples of good or bad character, on teacher advocacy of good conduct accompanied, at times, by utilization of extrinsic reinforcement to produce appropriate behavior, and on the inclusion of lessons with an explicit character theme. (p. 28)

Leming argued that another four programs—the Child Development Project, Project Essential, the Giraffe Program, and the Community of Caring program—appear to be derived from principles more consistent with the individual development orientation. These programs "place the major emphases on intrinsic motivation, on the classroom and school culture, on intrinsic reward structure, and on student discussion and problem solving" (Leming, 1997, p. 28). Leming further observes that other programs, especially the Heartwood Institute curriculum and the Character Education Curriculum, are eclectic in nature with regard to curricular orientation.

We now need to take a critical look at Leming's review. He fails to examine the so-called "objectives" of the character education programs, instead accepting character educators' claims that universal values exist and that good character consists of an individual manifesting behavioral outcomes. He stated, "Each character education objective on a given list is difficult to challenge" (p. 26), yet, in reality, the challenge is not difficult to pose and it must be done. Neither character educators nor Leming tell us how a given objective, or a value, is actually defined. They assume that all people conceptualize and approach any given value in the same way. However, this is not true. In real-life situations, any given value may have various definitions and interpretations. Different people may differ in their understanding of a specific value.

The situational and contextual nature of values, therefore, must be addressed. Different interpretations of values will result in different outcomes. Any given value may be taught in a way that contradicts a good intention. An educator's personal moral philosophy may affect his teaching just as a school's social culture and ideology may affect the collective efforts of character education.

Leming's (1997) conclusions seem to support the claims of character education leaders such as Lickona (1991, 1998) that character education is comprehensive in practice. The cognitive, affective, and behavioral aspects of character are promoted through a broad approach via the efforts of teachers, the academic curriculum, extracurricular activities, and the school culture in these programs. And the utilization of methods of intrinsic motivation and discussion, reflection, and problem solving indeed shows that character education seems to draw from multiple orientations and does not rely on mere didacticism.

Nevertheless, these character education programs still demonstrate that they are all virtue centered and, therefore, fall within one narrow orientation. Character, in these curricula, is exclusively defined in terms of virtue. A virtue is claimed to have objective existence, and the acquisition of virtue is the aim of character education. Acquiring virtue may require the cultivation of both mind and heart, and sometimes may require some individually oriented values and methods. But fundamentally the programs are still transmission oriented. The values are considered to be universal, ultimate, and objective truths, and the source of the truths, Western culture and history, goes unquestioned. No matter which pedagogical methods—exhortation or discussion, extrinsic reinforcement or intrinsic motivation—the goal is the same, to transmit those values to students and preserve the culture. This is the very nature of character education, and it sufficiently distinguishes itself from other truly individual development-oriented approaches to moral education such as the Kohlbergian approach and values clarification. Leming fails to critically examine this commonality among character education programs in his review.

As a supporter of the character education movement, Leming is mainly interested in the effectiveness of the pedagogical choices within the programs studied and does not critically examine the philosophical and ideological underpinnings of the entire movement. He accepts character educators' unfounded claim of the existence of universal values and avoids exploring more fundamental and complex issues related to their moral assumptions. He criticizes most programs for not having "a clear and explicit pedagogical perspective" but finds that "a general character education pedagogical model can be identified that at least half of the reviewed curricula share" (p. 29). The problem is that he introduces this model without offering any deeper analysis of it. He shows that the model is largely characterized by the direct teaching of values and uncritical behavioral training, yet he fails to examine the ideologies such as dogmatism and didacticism underlying this model.

National Schools of Character

In order to fully understand character education practice, we must examine another group of exemplary character education programs. This time we look at what the Character Education Partnership (CEP) offers us. As the largest organization promoting character education in the United States, the CEP sponsors the annual National Schools of Character Award program in order to disseminate model practices in character education to schools and districts across the nation.[2]

The main criteria used for screening applications and selecting the semifinalists and award winners are directly derived from the *Eleven Principles of Effective Character Education,* CEP's premier text for defining excellence in character education. In reviewing and assessing the individual schools or districts, the sponsor asks the following three questions of all applicants: (1) What are the goals of character education at your school or district? (2) How are you implementing character education in your school or district? and (3) How do you know you are successful?

In answering these questions, applicants are given the opportunity to explain how their school or district addressed the eleven principles. The 2000 National Schools of Character award winners include nine schools and one school district.[3] According to the program's publication:

> They [the award winners] adhere to a variety of educational philosophies and implement diverse instructional models....As a group they possess a number of commonalities. All of the National Schools of Character award winners exemplify principles set forth in the *Eleven Principles of Effective Character Education,* and all have experienced positive results from their character-building efforts. (CEP, 2000, pp. 7–8)

This statement clearly indicates that these model schools share certain patterns in their efforts. The links to the theories and guidelines created by the leaders of character education such as Lickona are explicit. In the rest of this chapter, I will discuss the program in two ways. First, I will summarize the common characteristics of these schools and their character education programs, after which, I will examine their links to the ideologies of the movement.

Common Features of the Model Schools
All these schools claim a commitment to promoting core ethical values in students. Setting goals is clearly emphasized by these schools. All schools agree upon a general goal, that character education is to be an integral part of their effort to develop students socially, ethically, and academically. They clearly acknowledge that intellectual or academic development is not the only goal of the school; the moral aspect must be stressed and integrated into the total educational process. All schools define character in terms of values and behaviors. Accordingly, they agree upon promoting core ethical values as their specific goal for character education. Each of these schools has developed a list of ethical values or character traits around which its entire approach to character education is centered. Core ethical values that appear on most of the lists include responsibility, respect, caring, fairness, integrity, compassion, cooperation, perseverance, courage, trustworthiness, and citizenship.

A common practice in the cultivation of these core values is the establishment of a connection between these values and the other goals of teaching and learning. Connections to academics and school discipline are especially stressed. For example, one elementary school emphasizes connecting positive character with "good academic habits" such as being enthusiastic about learning, evaluating one's own learning, and staying on task. Goals like listening attentively, following directions, and accepting responsibility for behavior are obviously linked to the school's requirement on student discipline. Thus, despite the non-contextual definition of the virtue in general, character education schools define and approach virtues based on particular contexts: Academics and discipline form the meanings of virtues.

Another commonality in these model schools is that they all emphasize strong leadership and staff involvement in character education. How is character education in a school launched? The principal's role is crucial, and it is usually the principal who initiates the character education program. But the principal is only part of the leadership group, the so-called "shared decision-making team." Each of these schools has a committee responsible for setting goals and planning activities for character education. The committee, usually composed of administrators, teachers, and support staff in the school, may sometimes reach out to parents and other community members for assistance in the decision-making process, but most important decisions are made within the committee. The most important job of the committee is to develop the list of core values or character traits to be focused on by curricula and school-wide activities. No information is given as to whether the committee is truly representative or whether the decision-making process is truly democratic.

The schools are recognized as models in their efforts to create a strong partnership among the school, home, and community. Character education in these schools is said to be a community effort. Schools claim to reach out to students' families and communities in order to establish and maintain a consensus on the goals of character development and conduct a joint, united effort to build students' character. Parental participation in activities is touted. Though some schools do get parents involved in their decision-making processes in character education, for the most part, parents and community members are just asked to support and assist in the implementation of the planned school efforts.

In terms of the specific issue of curriculum and instruction, these schools all emphasize infusing character education into the regular curriculum. Some schools create special classes on character education. These classes, usually given such titles as "Conflict Resolution" or "Healthy Choices," engage students in storytelling, journal writing, role-playing, discussions, and other activities to promote core values. These schools typically reject the idea that character education is a stand-alone and infuse character education across the regular curriculum. Social studies and language arts classes are emphasized as major vehicles for character education. However, even subjects such as music and physical education are expected to incorporate aspects of moral teaching.

Extracurricular activities also play an important role. Theme-related activities are common in all the schools. Most schools have the "one-virtue-per-month" program and organize activities around the virtue emphasized during the month. Guest speakers, community service, and charity activities are among many outside-of-the-classroom activities. Many schools work to establish traditional rituals and ceremonies such as flag raisings or annual school assemblies to carry on the spirit of character or values.

Student leadership is one of the most important vehicles for promoting good character at these schools, especially at the high school level. Student councils, student governments, and other student groups participate in the character education activities. For example, there is an annual student leadership conference at one high school, at which student representatives from every group in the school discuss character-related issues such as violence and conflict resolution.

These schools do not simply rely on special activities for character education; rather, they address character education across common routines on a daily basis. For example, teachers are encouraged to maintain a positive environment by conducting regular class meetings. The schools also work to establish a pro-character environment to shape a positive school culture, with the visual display of character traits on bulletin boards, posters, and banners a common practice.

The schools emphasize the role of examples. Teachers and staff are expected to act as role models for students by manifesting the desired character traits or core values and establishing and maintaining a character-building environment.

Finally, all the schools have awards for good character. Reward programs are popular in all the schools for recognizing students who exhibit good character traits. Awards such as "Student of the Month," "Outstanding Student of the Year," "Student of Responsibility," and "Student of Honesty" are common.

Raising Further Questions: The Linkages to Ideologies

A constructive critique of the character education programs must be dialectical in nature. Many efforts of the National Schools of Character are worthy of praise and encouragement. Educators in the model schools usually address the moral mission from two perspectives—that of moral education to counter social problems and that of holistic education. As argued in chapter 3, the first perspective is largely due to the misleading claims of moral decline in the literature, but the second perspective reflects not only a time-honored but also a currently important educational philosophy. Many teachers in these schools genuinely believe education is a holistic enterprise and embrace moral development and character building as an integral aim of teaching and schooling. Their commitment and dedication to moral education might be seen as positive and inspirational, especially in current American schools in which the pursuit of academic standards and the obsession with high-stakes testing dominate mainstream school culture. Unfortunately, character educators in these schools, like their leaders, promote the standards movement and make character education compatible with test imposition. As we have seen, the model schools connect strong character with "good academic habits" and use character education to improve student performance on high-stakes tests.

Character educators' emphasis on the partnership between school, home, and community represents the direction in which we should be headed. It is important to recognize moral education as the task of all the people involved in children's lives. This is especially so today when influences from the immediate environment and the larger society become increasingly complex and, very often, negative. Schools must meet the challenge of getting families and communities involved in education. Such an effort makes the environment more positive and educational. It must be noted, however, that community input or parental involvement does not necessarily produce the intended outcomes. The nature of the community or the parental involvement must be examined in the first place. A community that supports racism, for instance, cannot be trusted to help the school foster children's character.

At practical levels, the emphasis on the teachers' modeling is important, though heavy reliance on any given individual's example may cause other problems if that individual promotes a particular model of behavior or ideology. Integrating character education into the regular school curriculum and extracurricular activities is beneficial to students. Character educators' recognition of environment and school culture as mediators in character development is especially important, though much more work needs to be done in this regard. Although an embrace of multiple efforts and methods at first seems to reflect a rejection of moral didacticism and dogmatism, both still remain serious problems in current practice.

While giving credit to character educators, we must point out that although many schools conduct promising efforts, many of their strategies and practices raise serious questions.

What Is Missing from the List of Character Traits?
This question directly relates to character educators' moral philosophy, in other words, their fundamental assumptions regarding morality and moral education. Character education in the award-winning schools as well as in the exemplary programs Leming reviewed is virtue centered. Schools define good character as the possession and exhibition of the chosen character traits or core values. Every school organizes character education activities around a list of these traits or values. However, both the content of the list and the construction of the list are subject to close examination.

Respect, responsibility, caring, honesty, courage, etc., are defined as virtues. They are regarded as objective existences and even absolute entities. No inquiry is implemented to determine how a virtue is construed. No question is raised about how a virtue is contextualized. The virtue carries an absolute definition, but in specific school contexts, ironically, it is interpreted relatively. In these model schools virtues are typically defined as behavioral standards or rules to promote academic habits and maintain discipline. At one National School of Character, for example, "responsibility" is dismembered into "seven personal and social standards," including listening attentively, following directions, and staying on task. At another school, the Character Education Committee creates a "behavior matrix" representing the four character traits of responsibility, compassion, integrity, and respect. It details how students are expected to act in settings such as the lunchroom, the bathroom, outside the school, the office, the playground, the computer lab, and the hallway. A virtue is explained thus: "Integrity outside means being where you are supposed to be when you are supposed to be there and staying off playground equipment before and after school" (CEP, 2000, p. 27). One may wonder, is this building good character in school or training solders for the military?

In one of the schools, a teacher and character education committee member reports, "Most of the people in the committee were *trained* [italics added] in rubrics, and we believe the easiest way to communicate to kids what we expect is to show them *concretely* [italics added] what this behavior looks like" (CEP, 2000, p. 27). Character education is thus defined and practiced as behavior training. And the training is implemented as concretely and simply as possible. Developing character is superficially simplified as shaping good manners and conforming to rules. Fundamental and complex moral issues leave little room for exploration within character education. What a virtue like integrity really means for an individual person or a group of people in various contexts is ignored. When mere behavioral conformity is emphasized, moral reasoning and moral affect disappear. The knowledge, attitudes, ability, and skills needed for making important moral decisions in complex life situations are paid little attention.

It is evident that such practice is promoting particular ideologies in the name of absolute moral principles. Character educators claim virtues as absolute and universal but define and approach them within particular contexts. As a result, this formulation allows the influence and even control of certain ideologies to take over the school and students' lives. Leaders of character

Character Education in Practice 141

education, such as Wynne and Ryan (1997), would surely praise such a practice. They strongly argue for the behavioral training of students and urge students to be committed to academic study and school discipline without raising any critical questions regarding educational policies, such as the ones related to higher standards and high-stakes testing. Critical thinking is not encouraged under the authoritarianism represented by character education leaders' formula and these model schools of character.

What Is Wrong with the Community-Based Decision-Making Process?
Character educators claim to be democratic and community based. They emphasize community consensus on the creation of character traits or core values. As the National Schools of Character program shows, character education decision-making processes seem, on the surface, to be democratic. A committee of staff and teachers creates the virtue list and, apparently, sometimes garners some input from the community.

The seemingly community-based process shows some strengths. As introduced, such a process stresses strong leadership and partnership among the school, home, and community. It is important to recognize environmental influences on children's character development and invite relevant people to become involved in school character education efforts. However, such a process raises several problems that character educators do not seriously address.

The list of the so-called "universal values," "core values," or "common moralities" is mostly determined by a small group of adults within the school. The values are largely assumed by this small group to be either universal or community based. The committee may occasionally reach out to students and even get some community members involved in some decision-making processes, but the question remains whether the committee and its decisions are truly representative.

Character educators fail to address the issues of gender, race, class, and culture in the decision-making process. This is a major problem in the practice of character education. Gilligan (1982) and other feminist writers report that the moral development of girls differs considerably from that of boys. Anyon (1997), Delpit (1995), Ladson-Billings (1994), and Fine and Weis (1998, 2003) inform us of how issues of race, culture, and class pervade American schools and significantly affect children's personal lives and moral upbringing. These issues constitute the larger context of a child's moral development and character formation and, therefore, must be seriously considered in the decision-making process of any moral education initiative. Unfortunately, character educators often soften and trivialize these important issues in their claims of universality and community consensus in the teaching of a set of specific virtues or values.

A community does not always agree upon morally charged issues. As Noddings (2002) points out, it may be easy for a well-established community, one with recognized traditions and shared life styles, to come to a consensus on what it values. However, consensus will be more difficult to reach for a diverse group of parents and guardians who just happen to send their children to the same school. Thus, a concern naturally arises: Which subgroup will control the discussion during the decision-making process? Whose values will be taught? These are difficult but legitimate questions. Unfortunately, the exemplary programs and model schools avoid such central questions.

It is reasonable to point out that in the increasingly diverse American society, any pursuit of community consensus on the matters of morality might be too simplistic. Any claim of consensus on universal values might lack an honest moral ground. We have heard many such claims in the character education movement, but as discussed earlier, the claim of universality must be questioned. We doubt the moral ground of such a claim. The problem is that the voices and values of underprivileged groups may have been silenced or marginalized.

For example, the so-called effective schools researched and praised by Edward Wynne (1989b) espouse traditional Judeo-Christian values. However, the curricula and traditions imposed on all students could be offensive to many non-Judeo-Christian students and families. One might expect the minority to become vocal in opposition; some community members might even become morally outraged. If they do not speak out, we have to ask why. There may be several reasons. The school in question may be racially or culturally segregated; in other words, the school might be attended by predominantly white students of the same Judeo-Christian background, and Judeo-Christian teaching is not a problem for these students and families at all. Or, even if there is a significant number of minority students, the school might have successfully suppressed their perspectives. Or, if that is the case, minority students may accept the school's moral imposition in exchange for the other benefits the school provides. As we know, many inner-city non-Catholic parents send their children to Catholic schools and willingly accept a different worldview and religious instruction because they want the other benefits the school offers, including a relatively safe environment or a better academic reputation.

The National Schools of Character do not openly argue for the teaching of any particular religion-based morality and values. This must be considered a good disconnection between their character education practice and the theories of character education leaders. However, these character educators put themselves into another troubling situation: They have selected a common moral ground that, in actuality, may not exist. They must have realized the importance of welcoming all students from diverse backgrounds and opening schools to all religious faiths, but they wrongly claim an equal education to be the same education for all. By assuming that everyone accepts the list of character traits and by emphasizing that values are universally shared, they are still imposing an education stemming from particular ideologies on all students. They disguise their efforts with a neutral face, but it is a false neutrality because they are largely indifferent to the significant differences in students' moral notions and value choices, which flow from the diverse cultures and religions now being brought into schools. Character education is deceptively presented as racially, culturally, politically, and socially neutral. While commonalities are overestimated and differences overlooked, larger social, economic, cultural, and political issues are concealed. One of the most important aims of schooling, the promotion of social justice and equity, becomes trivialized.

The tendency to rely heavily on the community poses another problem. As Noddings (2002) warns us, "Character education requires a strong community but not necessarily a good one" (p. 7). In Chinese schools moral education was once dictated by the Communist Party in the name of the community and people and so contributed to communist control. One might worry that the emphasis on community in character education efforts in the United States may help create a highly moralistic but not necessarily moral schooling. In a moralistic school, one particular perspective of morality prevails while others are silenced or marginalized. It must be noted that although they emphasize community-based decision-making, character educators are likely to advocate and reinforce the ideologies and values of powerful and dominant social groups. The problem does not lie in the community-based decision-making per se; the problem is that community-based decision-making is rarely done, or, if done, it is superficial due to the fact that it is controlled by elites both within and outside of the school.

Is the Traditional Character Training Approach Effective?

Let us take a further look at the methods used in the programs. Character educators ignore Socrates' doubts about the possibility of direct teaching of virtues and instead embrace Aristotle's notions of the virtue ethics and the idea of training children in virtuous behaviors. From James Terry White in the early twentieth century to Thomas Lickona in the 1990s, character educators have always urged schools to directly teach students to know the good, love the good, and do the good. In the name of the so-called "comprehensive approach," traditional didactic pedagogy permeates the practice of character education.

Alfie Kohn (1997a) observes that "The great majority of character education programs consist largely of exhortation and direct recitation.... Their model of instruction is clear: good character or values are *instilled in* or *transmitted to* students" (p. 158). The National Schools of Character indeed utilize many traditional methods of character training such as the visual display, enumeration, memorization, and recitation of virtues in the forms of creeds, verses, slogans, and golden texts; imitation of heroes and role models; and reward and punishment of certain behaviors.

Even some advocates for character education are concerned about, and critical of, this approach. In a commentary on character education, three CEP officers, Eric Schaps, Esther F. Schaeffer, and Sanford N. McDonnell (2001) worry that "too many programs...are aimed mostly at promoting good manners and compliance with rules, not at developing students of strong, independent character" (p. 40).[4] They put problematic character education programs into four groups—"cheerleading," "praise and reward," "define and drill," and "forced formality." Often these approaches are used in combination with one another. Their descriptions of these varieties are vivid, pointing out the many problematic mentalities underlying these approaches.[5] Under the popular one-virtue-per-month approach, for example, the memorization of definitions of the virtues is equated with the development of the far more complex capacity for moral reasoning. A diet of upbeat moral messages is expected to produce a long-standing commitment to becoming a moral person. As the reward or award becomes the primary focus and the real significance of the students' actions is lost, character education creates quick behavioral results but not deep moral commitment, sincere moral emotion, or the ability and skills needed for moral decision-making in real life's complex situations. Schaps, Schaeffer, and McDonnell target the very problems we find in the National Schools of Character, yet, ironically, these

Character Education in Practice 145

model schools are selected and rewarded by the CEP, where these three authors serve as directors and officers.

Educators in the National Schools of Character are content with what they are doing and what they have achieved. In their literature, these schools proudly announce such major "achievements" resulting from character education as higher standardized testing scores, fewer office referrals and discipline issues, orderly student behavior in open areas, and a more comfortable school environment. The schools use statistics to justify their claims of success. As one school reports, "Character education has had a *quantifiable* [italics added] effect on the school climate and academic results" (CEP, 2000, p. 25).

It is an open question as to whether character and morality can be quantitatively measured. Moreover, the question is whether character educators are really measuring character and morality. What is the actual connection between character and academic achievement? Does a score increase on a standardized test reflect a good character? What is the relationship between character and discipline? Why does the fact that "office referrals have declined 60 percent" (CEP, 2000, p. 25) indicate an improvement in character, particularly in the sense of personal growth and maturity? In many Chinese schools where extremely oppressive adult control is practiced, office referral is zero. Can we assume that a healthy and strong student character grows in that environment?

In short, it is doubtful that current practices in character education promote good character and moral people as character educators pledge to do and even may strive to do. Even the three officers of CEP recognize the serious limitations of the practice. What many schools do "may well produce certain limited benefits, such as calling attention to matters of character or bringing some order to a chaotic environment. But they will not yield deep and enduring effects on character" (Schaps, Schaeffer, and McDonnell, 2001, p. 40). As Hartshorne and May (1928–1930) warned educators a long time ago, moralizing to children or giving them direct instruction in moral principles makes little difference in children's moral lives.

In the process of exhortation and direct recitation of specific yet largely meaningless virtues, critical thinking is seriously ignored. There is no empowerment of students. Indoctrination is legitimated. Actually, as we have seen from the works of writers such as Bennett and Wynne, indoctrination is not viewed as necessarily bad. Devaluing the nondirective nature of the moral reasoning approach, the leaders of character education overlook Kohlberg's thoughtful criticism of traditional character education as indoctrination. And now as we see, character educators in practice consciously and unconsciously embrace indoctrination.

Such a pedagogical orientation is consistent with certain dominant ideologies such as behaviorism and religious dogmatism. Character educators reject behaviorism at the theoretical level as they claim to promote human values. However, they hold the premise that children need to be fixed just as behaviorists do and uncritically use many strategies characteristic of behaviorism, such as explicit training and the use of reward and punishment.

Unlike behaviorists who view the child as a tabula rasa, without an inherent nature and thus shaped by the environment, character educators have a strikingly dark view of children's nature. This is explicitly indicated by the arguments of Kilpatrick and Wynne. Based on such a dark view, character educators emphasize the teaching of self-control (make children do what they are told and work hard) and other distinctly conservative values. Here again, the connection between character education and religion emerges. The dark view of human nature is akin to the conception of original sin, a conception promoted by the Judeo-Christian traditions. These religions hold a belief that human nature is originally flawed and that for personal salvation, individuals need to engage in nonstop self-discipline and self-cultivation under external rules. Rigid discipline and training are well advocated by character education proponents.

In summary, despite the apparent and sometimes striking variations, common patterns, or themes, indeed exist in character education programs. Emphasizing the transmission of the so-called universal values, claiming to be democratic and community-based, and embracing moralizing and direct instruction in behavioral training, character educators promote the theories and ideologies of the leaders of the movement. Absolutism, authoritarianism, dogmatism, behaviorism, and conservatism are explicitly and implicitly shaping the movement. These political ideologies are driving the realities of character education.

Notes

1. The ten programs are listed below:
    (1) AEGIS: Acquiring Ethical Guidelines for Individual Development, a K-6 character education program developed by the Institute for Research and Evaluation in Salt Lake City, Utah, in 1996.

Character Education in Practice

(2) Character Education Curriculum: A curriculum developed by the Character Education Institute in 1996 in San Antonio, Texas.
(3) The Child Development Project: A K-6 character education program developed in 1996 by the Developmental Studies Center in Oakland, California, with an initial grant from the Hewlett Foundation.
(4) Community of Caring: A program developed by Community of Caring, Inc., in Washington, D.C., and supported by the Joseph P. Kennedy, Jr. Foundation in 1996.
(5) Project Essential: A K-12 curriculum developed by the Teel Institute for the Development of Integrity and Ethical Behavior in Kansas City, Missouri, in 1996.
(6) An Ethics Curriculum for Children: A literature-based elementary-level character education program developed by the Heartwood Institute in Pittsburgh, Pennsylvania, in 1992.
(7) The Giraffe Program: A K-12 program defined as a character education and service-learning curriculum by developers in Washington in 1996.
(8) Lessons in Character: A K-5 character education curriculum developed in 1996 in San Diego, California, which draws on the "Six Pillars of Character" of the Character Counts Coalition.
(9) Lions-Quest: Skills for Growing: A K-5 curriculum developed by Quest International in 1990 in Newark, Ohio.
(10) The Responsive Classroom: A curriculum developed by the Northeast Foundation for Children in 1991 in Greenfield, Massachusetts. (see Leming, 1997, for a detailed description of these programs.)

2. The CEP administered and publicized the 2000 program with the support of grants from the John Templeton Foundation and the UAW-GM Center for Human Resources. CEP also received assistance from the Center for the Advancement of Ethics and Character (CAEC) at Boston University in defining and carrying out the awards program. Together, CEP and CAEC created the Blue Ribbon Panel of experts in the field of character education, developing the selection criteria and making the final selection of the National Schools of Character award winners.

3. The 2000 award-winning schools and one district are listed below:
Columbine Elementary School (Pre-K-5) in Woodland Park, Colorado
Cotswold Elementary School (K-5) in Charlotte, North Carolina
Emperor Elementary School (K-6) in San Gabriel, California
Excelsior Academy (4-12) in San Diego, California
Kennerly Elementary School (K-5) in St. Louis, Missouri
Longfellow Elementary School (K-6) in Hastings, Nebraska
Morgan Road Elementary School (K-6) in Liverpool, New York
Mt. Lebanon School District (K-12) in Pittsburgh, Pennsylvania
South Carroll High School (9-12) in Sykesville, Maryland
Walnut Hill Elementary School (Pre-K-6) in Dallas, Texas

4. Eric Schaps is the current president of the Character Education Partnership in Washington, D.C., and the founder and president of the Developmental Studies Center in Oakland, California. Esther F. Schaeffer is the executive director and chief executive officer of CEP, and Sanford N. McDonnell is its founder and chairman of the board.

5. Schaps, Schaeffer, and McDonnell describe the characteristics of these approaches. The cheerleading variety involves multicolored posters, banners, and bulletin boards featuring a value or virtue of the month; lively morning public-address announcements; occasional motivational assemblies; and possibly a high-profile event such as a fund-raiser for a good cause. The praise-and-reward approach seeks to make virtue into habits in the same way that B. F. Skinner used food pellets to shape the behavior of rats and pigeons. "Positive reinforcement" is its mainstay, often in the form of "catching students being good" and praising them or giving them chits that can be exchanged for privileges or prizes. Another hallmark is awards assemblies, during which a few selected students are publicly extolled for being, say, particularly helpful or courteous. In the define-and-drill approach, students are called on to memorize a list of values and the definition of each. Teachers quiz students: "Class, what do we mean by honesty? Respect? Integrity?" in the same manner that they ask, "What's eight times seven? Four times nine?" In the forced-formality approach, a school focuses its character education efforts on strict, uniform compliance with specific rules of conduct. It may emphasize, for example, certain kinds of hall behavior (walking in lines, arms at one's sides), or formal forms of address ("yes sir," "no ma'am), or other procedures deemed to promote order or respect (standing when any adult enters the room).

CHAPTER SIX

Back to the Future: Alternative Moral Education and School Reform

In October 2001, the central committee of the Chinese Communist Party issued *The Citizens' Guide for Moral Construction*. This imperial edict on moral education is the Party's new effort to address the growing social problems facing China as the country undergoes further economic reform. The Party expects the guide to help restore law and order across society, but that is unlikely to occur, as many of the problems, such as crimes and corruption, are rooted in the country's socioeconomic transition. During this time of transition, the failures in national policies have resulted in such tribulations as increasing poverty among working-class people and the concentration of political power within a few social groups. As this document indicates, the Party continues to circumvent the more sensitive political and social issues while emphasizing individual morality.

An international comparison helps us better understand the problems in the United States. After all, the Enron and WorldCom scandals are in many ways similar to those grave economic crimes in China. Then the question arises: Who is degrading the moral fabric of America? Those alienated boys and poor minorities that character education leaders, such as Bennett, target or these energy and communication giants? This is not about who is worse and who deserves more blame. This is about tracing the root of the problems and asking who has the greater political and economic power to keep things the same or change them for the better of all. Moral/character education advocates in both countries seem to focus on the powerless, the weak, and the deprived, unfairly holding them responsible for the creation and maintenance of a moral society. Meanwhile, they cast a blind eye on those who control the capital resources and make final decisions.

This has been a common scenario in the history of both countries. Whenever society entered a critical period (usually a transition time) and the ruling class faced challenges, moral education was called upon to make a difference. As the historical and contemporary analyses in chapters 2 and 3 illustrate, the introduction and reintroduction of character education in the United States coincided with two critical periods in the history of American capitalism. When the economy was in trouble and the social order was shaky, the issues of motivation, responsibility, and self-discipline were brought up by business and political leaders. Personality-related problems were exaggerated and moral education overemphasized. When schools and families became scapegoats for social problems, the failures of socioeconomic and political systems were trivialized.

Character education advocates are more concerned with maintaining the existing social order and traditional morality than with addressing the root causes of social problems such as violence and drug abuse. The leaders of the U.S. character education movement, such as Bennett, Kilpatrick, Wynne, Lickona, and Ryan, explicitly or implicitly called upon the schools to preserve the dominant white Anglo-Saxon culture rather than educate youth to become critical citizens who can actively engage in social change and cultural transformation.

Character education's linkages to the past are significant. White's (1909) misconstruction of social problems as individual moral decay was resurrected in the 1980s and 1990s by Bennett and Lickona. The theoretical framework of character education prescribed by these modern leaders is strikingly similar to that formulated in the early twentieth century. Direct teaching of virtues is defined as the core of character building. As Bennett and his followers themselves explicitly claim, such a core is nothing more than what was promoted in the past. They simply want to continue the tradition. In practice, character educators, following the guidelines of their leaders, develop a virtue-centered moral training approach. Neither the list of character traits nor the set of curricular and extracurricular activities designed for character education is in nature different from what early character educators created. Attempting to be innovative, character educators today claim to teach universal virtues and engage in democratic and community-based decision-making. However, in reality, they largely ignore issues of gender, race, class, and culture that decidedly affect individuals' moral lives and deceptively present character education as politically neutral. While claiming to be committed to absolute moral principles, they define and approach virtues based on neo-conservative ideologies and make relative recommendations to students.

In the name of a so-called comprehensive approach, character educators allow traditional didactic pedagogy to permeate their practice. Because character education today is basically repeating the same practices utilized in the early twentieth century, we are likely to come to the same conclusion that Hartshorne and May (1928–1930) drew, namely, that in practical terms, character education is woefully inadequate and ineffective. Moralizing to children or giving them direct instruction in moral principles makes little difference in their moral lives. Character education may well produce certain limited benefits such as quick behavioral changes and a less-chaotic environment. However, it is unlikely to yield deep and enduring effects on character.

Given its many serious weaknesses, character education does not represent an encouraging direction for school reform. The overall national school reform movement continues to be content oriented, standards based, and test driven. Such a reform agenda has been seriously criticized, especially by those advocating a structural reform of American schools (see Apple, 1996, Kohn, 1999, Noddings, 1992). As critics argue, the move toward uniformity in standards, curriculum, and assessment, though seemingly favoring academic development of children, is anti-intellectual in nature and discourages critical thinking, creativity, and novelty in teaching and learning. In addition, the agenda seriously ignores the cultural diversity in American schools and undermines democracy in education. As Apple (1996) points out, "…behind the educational justifications for a national curriculum and national testing is an ideological attack that is very dangerous. Its effects will be truly damaging to those who already have the most to lose in this society" (p. 24).

Character education promotes the standards-based school reform. Bennett, Wynne, and Lickona have been outspoken advocates for this overall school reform movement. They support educational policies that promote academic standards, a national curriculum, and high-stakes testing and make character education theoretically compatible with these initiatives. In practice, character educators typically define virtues in terms of academic habits and training children to be "good' students in accordance with the standards. Schools typically use character education to maintain order and discipline.

There are deep connections between the standards movement and character education. The idea of the "common culture," defined in terms of Western standards and values by Bennett (1992) and his allies, is the very basis upon which these reform agendas are built. Within the framework of this common culture, traditional knowledge and moral values, authority, standards, national identity, and market-driven principles are interwoven and emphasized. As the standards movement largely promotes the cultural politics of conservative power elites, character education reinforces their ideological control of values in American schools.

In short, connected to a larger movement of conservative restoration, the overall school reform agenda does not challenge the fundamental school structure as the source of problems; therefore, it cannot bring significant and positive changes to American education. Similarly, character education, although it might have been expected by some to lessen the obsession with academics and tests, only reinforces the status quo and steers school reform in the wrong direction.

Leming (2001/2002) argues, "It's impossible to characterize this movement [the character education movement] as a right-wing conspiracy" (p. 9). A simplistic politicization of character education as either Right or Left indeed not only misreads the good intentions of many character educators but also misinterprets the political nature of the movement. The political nature of character education is not determined by its advocates but by its underlying ideologies. As Purpel (1999) points out, the movement, "far from being innovative and reforming, represents instead a long-standing tradition of using schools as agents of social stability, political stasis, and cultural preservation" (p. 83). Character education, despite variations in its theories and practices, essentially promotes conservative ideologies such as authoritarianism, absolutism, and religious dogmatism. Entangled with and even controlled by these ideologies, character education can hardly achieve its promised goals of moral development and character building.

Transformative school reform is needed. Alternative moral education is required. Developing such an alternative is beyond the scope of this book, and, to be consistent with the central argument made throughout this book, any grand narratives about moral education must be rejected. For that reason, the following discussion on alternative moral education will remain brief, eclectic, and open ended. It will focus on several key issues that have emerged throughout the political and ideological analysis—how moral education addresses the relationships between the child and the curriculum and between the individual and the society, how moral education involves socialization, how moral education deals with both absolutism and relativism, and how moral education relates to other aspects of schooling.

A dialectical notion is needed to understand how moral education should address the relationships between the child and the curriculum and between the individual and society. John Dewey's ideas are most insightful. Any curriculum, including a moral education program, must be organized around the child's developmental needs and life experiences. As Dewey (1902/1974) argues, "The child is the starting-point, the center, and the end. His development, his growth, is the ideal. It alone furnishes the standard" (p. 343). The child must be appreciated as the moral subject who has a moral identity to be developed and a moral framework to be improved in school. He is not an empty vessel to be filled with external moral influences (in the forms of virtues, morals, values, examples, models, and the like), nor is he a piece of clay passively waiting to be molded by educators into a certain preferred type.

The complexity of the child's moral life must be considered (Coles, 1986). All dimensions of morality, including moral energy, knowledge, belief, imagination, reasoning, judgments, feelings, and actions, should be the concerns of moral education. All relational aspects of a child's life, such as home, school, community, work, study, and leisure, should be emphasized in character building. The child's social, economic, ethnic, racial, and cultural background matters most for his character formation; therefore, moral education must involve a constant inquiry and exploration into these essential issues. They cannot be softened, neutralized, or trivialized in the name of pursuing a so-called universality or commonality in the teaching of a set of specific moral virtues. Apple's (1996) argument for a democratic curriculum and pedagogy is also helpful toward this end. A democratic program in moral education must also "begin with a recognition of 'the different social positionings and cultural repertoires in the classrooms, and the power relations between them'" (p. 33).

Moral education centering on the child's needs and life does not require separation from society. Moral life is grounded in social life, with the social giving meaning to the individual. "Here individualism and socialism are at one" (Dewey, 1899/1974, p. 295). Socialization deserves a place in moral education. However, moral education must also move beyond blind socialization. No social life is fixed, nor should it be fixed. The nature of socialization in any particular context must be subject to examination. Schools are not entitled to be the uncritical transmitters of the traditional values of any given society or culture. The young should be prepared not only to adapt to the various demands of the society but also to challenge the status quo and change it. A critical inquiry of our tradition and heritage better serves to preserve and extend what we cherish as a people. Producing mere servants of the society is not the real purpose of moral education, while educating active agents of human liberation and social betterment is its goal.

To avoid both absolutism and relativism, morality and moral education must be understood as situational and context based. Virtues and values may be taught, but they must be taught critically and situated within contexts. They cannot be defined as a set of prescribed and fixed rules or norms external to the child's actual life. Free choice and reasoning must be encouraged for rational moral decision-making. In this regard, values clarification and the cognitive-developmental approach still have a lot to offer despite their respective serious weaknesses.

It is obvious that character educators see morality as an individual matter. On the contrary, we must emphasize the relational or public nature of morality. Virtues are not individual possessions. Character building does not stop at the recitation of context-free moral traits or codes. Moral education is more than what is done in the one-virtue-per-month model. The inculcation of virtues is unlikely to produce virtuous people. Moral education is more about creating a condition and a process in which the moral life can flourish. In this regard, Nel Noddings's works have been instrumental. As she maintains, building conditions and relationships that support moral ways of life is more important than the inculcation of virtues in students (Noddings, 2002). She constructs an alternative approach to moral education based on an ethic of care. Unlike character educators, Noddings moves caring from an admirable trait of individual character to a necessary cultural condition. Such a caring condition must be created throughout various relationships within a child's life, such as the relationships between the child and the teacher, the child and his family and peers, the child and the subject matter, and the child and the environment.

Context-based and process-oriented moral education does not arise from an add-on program. It requires restructuring schools. Schooling today in many places is countering child development in general and moral development in particular. We must fight against poverty, racism, and the resulting "savage inequalities" (Kozol, 1992) evident in so many schools. A school system like the one Kozol visited in East St. Louis is morally deplorable; imposing any moral education program upon the dispossessed children in that school system is not only hypocritical but exacerbates the gap between the haves and have-nots. Many other school practices need to be critically examined as well. These practices include the differential tracking system, the impersonal zero-tolerance policy, and the excessive high-stakes testing, among others. Ironically, the testing fever is even inducing an increase in immoral behaviors, as cheating scandals by both students and teachers have demonstrated. Moral education must challenge these established and emerging practices and make the entire school structure, school culture, and educational process morally justifiable and defendable.

A progressive moral education approach could be created with careful and constructive consideration of these important issues. Such an alternative approach might not be politically and ideologically neutral, but it is by design politically and ideologically sensitive. After all, politics and ideologies are topics in moral education to be explored, and such exploration will contribute to the education of children to be active agents of genuine moral maturation, human liberation, and social improvement.

An eclectic effort is important in drawing upon what theorists and researchers have achieved in the field. As the analysis in this book shows, each of the existing theories of moral education has particular strengths. For example, we still need the values clarification proponents' recognition of the child as the moral subject and their emphasis on the child's valuing process in moral education. Kohlberg's cognitive-developmental approach rightfully highlights moral reasoning and moral decision-making. Noddings's caring alternative emphasizes creating the culture of caring that is so urgently needed today. These major theories should be regarded as the starting points in the development of new alternatives. Therefore, they must be more carefully and constructively evaluated.

We can even learn from character education itself. Character educators' appreciation of tradition and community, their use of stories and examples, and their emphasis on behavioral formation could be construed in a more balanced and less assertive/extreme way. We need to have a healthy respect for virtues and their development, which character educators distinctly emphasize, even if we cannot adopt their non-contextualized definition of virtues and their belief in direct inculcation.

Moral education as a subset of education is closely interrelated to other aspects of education, and its effective implementation requires a truly holistic view of the purpose of schooling and a structural reform in teaching and learning. Any moral education effort must be accompanied by the restructuring of schools. The relationship between moral education and school reform is thus an important issue to be explored. More in-depth studies are needed to examine more specific issues, such as those regarding moral education and the standards movement, moral education and high-stakes testing, moral edu-

education and tracking systems, moral education and school bureaucracy, moral education and cultural diversity, and moral education and youth deviance/youth culture.

Finally, to repeat the central message permeating this book, I must emphasize that a social and political critique is important for the examination of any issues related to education in general and moral education in particular. Ideologies and politics underlie educational ideals and theories and shape educational policies and practices. They fundamentally affect our understanding of education as both a moral and political enterprise. It is our obligation to engage in such a dialectical critique.

References

Adler, P. A., & Adler, P. (Eds.) (2000). *Constructions of deviance: Social power, contexts, and interaction* (third ed.). Belmont, CA: Wadsworth.

Anderson, D. (1998). Curriculum, culture, and community: The challenge of school violence. In M. Tonry & M. Moore (Eds.), *Youth violence* (pp. 317–364). Chicago: The University of Chicago Press.

Anyon, J. (1980). Social class and the hidden curriculum of work. *Journal of Education, 162,* 67–92.

———. (1997). *Ghetto schooling: A political economy of urban educational reform.* New York: Teachers College Press.

Apple, M. W. (1996). *Cultural politics and education.* New York: Teachers College Press.

Bai, L. (1998). Monetary reward versus the national ideological agenda: Career choice among Chinese university students. *Journal of Moral Education, 27* (4), 525–540.

Banks, J. A. (Ed.) (1996). *Multicultural education, transformative knowledge, and action: Historical and contemporary perspectives.* New York: Teachers College Press.

Becker, H. (2000). Labeling theory. In P. Adler & P. Adler (Eds.), *Constructions of deviance* (pp. 78–82). Belmont, CA: Wadsworth.

———. (2000). Moral entrepreneurs. In P. Adler & P. Adler (Eds.), *Constructions of deviance* (pp.139–146). Belmont, CA: Wadsworth.

Bennett, W. J. (1992). *The de-valuing of America: The fight for our culture and our children.* New York: Summit Books.

———. (Ed.) (1993). *The book of virtues: A treasury of great moral stories.* New York: Simon & Schuster.

———. (1994). *The index of leading cultural indicators: Facts and figures on the state of American society.* New York: Simon & Schuster.

Bennett, W. J., & Delattre E. J. (1978). Moral education in schools. *The Public Interest, 50,* 81–102.

Bennett, W. J., Dilulio, J. J. Jr., & Walters, J. P. (1996). *Body count: Moral poverty...and how to win America's war against crime and drugs.* New York: Simon & Schuster.

Bennetta, W. J. (1994). Lickona promotes false claims about sex education. *Educational Leadership, 52* (2), 74–75.

Benninga, J. A. (1997). Schools, character development, and citizenship. In A. Molnar (Ed.), *The construction of children's character* (pp. 77–96). Chicago: The University of Chicago Press.

Berlak, Harold. (2002). Academic achievement, race, and reform: A short guide to understanding assessment policy, standardized achievement tests, and anti-racist alternatives. Retrieved Jan. 2002 from http://www.edjustice.org.

Berliner, D., & Biddle, B. (1995). *The manufactured crisis: Myths, fraud, and the attack on America's public schools.* New York: Addison-Wesley.

Best, J. (2001, May 4). Telling the truth about damned lies and statistics. *The Chronicle of Higher Education*, p. B7.

Bloom, A. (1987). *The closing of the American mind*. New York: Simon & Schuster.

Bowles, S., & Gintis, H. (1976). *Schooling in capitalist America: Educational reform and the contradictions of economic life*. New York: Basic Books.

Chapman, W. E. (1969). *Roots of character education: An exploration of the American heritage from the decade of the 1920s*. Schenectady, NY: Character Research Press.

Character Education Partnership. (2000). *2000 national schools of character*. Washington, DC: Character Education Partnership.

Chazan, B. (1985). *Contemporary approaches to moral education: Analyzing alternative theories*. New York: Teachers College Press.

Chomsky, N. (1999). *The new military humanism: Lessons from Kosovo*. Monroe, ME: Common Courage Press.

———. (2000). *Rogue state: The rule of force in world affairs*. Cambridge, MA: South End Press.

———. (2001). *9-11*. New York: Seven Stories Press.

Coles, R. (1986). *The moral life of children*. Boston: Houghton Mifflin.

Commission on the Reorganization of Secondary Education (1918). Cardinal principles of secondary education. *Department of the Interior, Bureau of Education Bulletin*, No. 35. Washington, D C.: United States Government Printing Office.

Connell, W. (1976). Moral education: Aims and methods in China, the U.S.S.R., the U.S., and England. In D. Purpel & K. Ryan (Eds.), *Moral education…it comes with the territory* (pp. 30–43). Berkeley, CA: McCutchan.

Counting the human cost: A survey of projects counting civilians killed by the war in Iraq. (June 12, 2003). Retrieved June 20, 2003 from http://www.iraqbodycount.net.

Currie, E. (1993, November). *Missing pieces: Notes on crime, poverty, and social policy*. Paper presented for the Social Science Research Council's Committee for Research on the Urban Underclass, Policy Conference on Persistent Urban Poverty, Washington, D.C.

Damon, W. (Ed.) (2002). *Bringing in a new era in character education* (Hoover Books Online). Available at http://www-hoover.stanford.edu/publications/books.html.

Delpit, L. (1995). *Other people's children: Cultural conflict in the classroom*. New York: The New Press.

Devine, T., & Wilson, A (2000). *Cultivating hearts and character in the home, school, and community*. New York: International Educational Foundation.

Dewey, J. (1909). *Moral principles in education*. Boston: Houghton Mifflin.

———. (1934). *A common faith*. New Haven, CT: Yale University Press.

———. (1974). Ethical principles underlying education. In R. D. Archambault (Ed.), *John Dewey on education* (pp. 108–138). Chicago: The University of Chicago Press (original work published 1897).

———. (1974). The school and society. In R. D. Archambault (Ed.), *John Dewey on education* (pp. 295–310). Chicago: The University of Chicago Press (original work published 1899).

References

———. (1974). The child and the curriculum. In R. D. Archambault (Ed.), *John Dewey on education* (pp. 339–358). Chicago: The University of Chicago Press (original work published 1902).

Diaz, C. F. (2001). *Multicultural education for the twenty-first century.* New York: Longman.

Durkheim, E. (2000). The normal and the pathological. In P. Adler & P. Adler (Eds.), *Constructions of deviance* (pp. 53–57). Belmont, CA: Wadsworth.

Education Secretary blames shootings in schools on "alienation," not guns. Retrieved March 12, 2001, from http://www.sltnb.com/03122001/nation_w/78935.htm.

Erikson, K. (2000). On the sociology of deviance. In P. Adler & P. Alder (Eds.), *Constructions of deviance* (pp.11–18). Belmont CA: Wadsworth.

Federal Interagency Forum on Child and Family Statistics. (2002). *America's children: Key national indicators of well-being, 2002.* Retrieved July 12, 2002, from http: //www.childstats.gov.

Fine, M. (1997). Witnessing whiteness. In M. Fine, L. Weis, L. C. Powell, and L. M. Wong (Eds.), *Off white: Readings on race, power, and society* (pp. 57–65). New York: Routledge.

Fine, M., & Weis, L. (1998). *The unknown city: Lives of poor and working-class young adults.* Boston: Beacon Press.

———. (2003). *Silenced voices and extraordinary conversations: Re-imagining schools.* New York: Teachers College Press.

Gallup, G. H. (1975). The seventh annual Gallup poll of public attitudes toward the public schools. *Phi Delta Kappan, 57,* 227–241.

———. (1980). The twelfth annual Gallup poll of public attitudes toward the public schools. *Phi Delta Kappan, 62,* p. 39.

Garbarino, J. (1995). *Raising children in a socially toxic environment.* San Francisco: Jossey-Bass.

———. (1999). *Lost boys: Why our sons turn violent and how we can save them.* New York: The Free Press.

Gilligan, C. (1982). *In a different voice: Psychological theory and women's development.* Cambridge, MA: Harvard University Press.

Giroux, H. (1988). Teachers as intellectuals. Granby, MA: Bergin & Garvey.

——— (1992). *Border crossings: Cultural workers and the politics of education.* New York: Routledge.

———. (1997). *Channel surfing: Racism, the media, and the destruction of today's youth.* New York: St. Martin's Griffin.

———. (2000). Representations of violence, popular culture, and demonization of youth. In S. U. Spina (Ed.), *Smoke and mirrors: The hidden context of violence in schools and society* (pp. 93–105). Lanham, MD: Rowman & Littlefield.

Gonzalez, R. (2002). Ignorance is not bliss. Retrieved January 2, 2002, from http://www.sfgate.com

Gross, S. R., & Mauro, R. (1988). *Death and discrimination: Racial disparities in capital sentencing.* Boston: Northeastern University Press.

Hartshorne, H., & May, M. (1928–1930). *Studies in the nature of character* (Vols. 1–3). New York: Macmillan.

———. (1975). *Studies in the nature of character. Vol. I: Studies in deceit. Book One: General methods and results*. New York: Arno Press (original work published 1928).

Harvard Civil Rights project. Racial inequity in special education. Retrieved June 2002 from http://www.civilrightsproject.harvard.edu/research/specialed/IDEA_paper02.php.

Haynes, C. C. (2000, October 28). Let character education be an initiative in schools. *Press & Sun-Bulletin*, p. 3B.

Hirsch, E. D. (1987). *Cultural literacy: What every American needs to know*. Boston: Houghton Mifflin.

Hsieh, C. C., & Pugh, M. D. (1993). Poverty, income, inequality, and violent crime: A meta-analysis of recent aggregate data studies. *Criminal Justice Review, 18* (2), 182–202.

Hutchins, W. (1917). *Children's code of morals for elementary schools*. Washington, D C: Character Education Institution.

Jackson, D. (1989, January 23). Police embody racism to my people. *The New York Times.*

Jiang, Z. (2000, February 1). Guanyu jiaoyu wenti de tanhua [A speech on education]. *Zhongguo Jiaoyu Bao*, p.1.

Katz, M. B. (1971). *Class, bureaucracy, and schools: The illusion of educational change in America*. New York: Praeger.

Kempf, K. L. & Austin, R. L. (1986). Older and more recent evidence on racial discrimination in sentencing. *Journal of Quantitative Criminology* (2), 29–48.

Kilpatrick, W. K. (1992). *Why Johnny can't tell right from wrong*. New York: Simon & Schuster.

Kliebard, H. M. (1995). *The struggle for American curriculum: 1893–1958* (second ed.). New York: Routledge.

Kohlberg, L. (1975). Moral education for a society in moral transition. *Educational Leadership, 33* (1), 46–54.

Kohn, A. (1992). *No contest: The case against competition*. Boston: Houghton Mifflin.

———. (1997a). The trouble with character education. In A. Molnar (Ed.), *The construction of children's character* (pp. 154–162). Chicago: The University of Chicago Press.

———. (1997b). How not to teach values: A critical look at character education. *Phi Delta Kappan, 78* (6), 428–439.

———. (1999). *The schools our children deserve: Moving beyond traditional classrooms and "tougher standards."* Boston: Houghton Mifflin.

———. (2000). *The case against standardized testing*. Portsmouth, NH: Heinemann.

Kozol, J. (1992). *Savage inequalities: Children in America's schools*. New York: Harper Perennial.

Ladson-Billings, G. (1994). *The dreamkeepers: Successful teachers of African American children*. San Francisco: Jossey-Bass.

Leland, J. (1999, May 10). The secret life of teens. *Newsweek*, 44–50.

Leming, J. S. (1993). In search of effective character education. *Educational Leadership*, 51, 63–71.

———. (1997). Whither goes character education? Objectives, pedagogy, and research in education programs. *Journal of Education, 179* (2), 11–34.

References

———. (2001, Fall/2002, Winter). Character education: New push has old roots. *School of Education News, The Newsletter of the University of Wisconsin-Madison School of Education,* p. 9.

Lickona, T. (1991). *Educating for character: How our schools can teach respect and responsibility.* New York: Bantam Books.

———. (1993). The return of character education. *Educational Leadership, 51* (3), 6–11.

———. (1996). The decline and fall of American civilization: Can character education reverse the slide? *Currents in Modern Thoughts,* June 1996, 285–307.

———. (1997). Educating for character: A comprehensive approach. In A. Molnar (Ed.), *The construction of children's character* (pp. 45–62). Chicago: The University of Chicago Press.

———. (1998). A more complex analysis is needed. *Phi Delta Kappan, 79* (6), 449–454.

———. (1999). Religion and character education. *Phi Delta Kappan, 81* (1), 21–27.

Lickona, T., Schaps, E., & Lewis, C. (1995). *Eleven principles of effective character education.* Washington, DC: Character Education Partnership.

Lu, H. (2003). Low-income children in the United States. Retrieved October 26, 2003, from http://www.nccp.org.

Lu, J. (2000). Ren dui ren de lijie: Daode jiaoyu de jichu [Mutual understanding among human beings: Basis of moral education]. *Jiaoyu Yanjiu, 21* (7), 3–10, 54.

Luksetich, W. A., & White, M. D. (1982). *Crime and public policy: An economic approach.* Boston and Toronto: Little, Brown and Company.

Mao, T. (1977). How to deal with the internal contradictions among the people. In *Collective works of Mao Tzetung* (Vol. 5). Beijing: People's Press (original work published 1957).

McClellan, B. E. (1999). *Moral education in America: Schools and the shaping of character from colonial times to the present.* New York: Teachers College Press.

McKown, H. C. (1935). *Character education.* New York: McGraw-Hill.

Mendez, G. A. (1983). *The role of race and ethnicity in the incidence of police use of deadly force.* New York: National Urban League.

Ministry of Education. (2000). 2000 jiaoyubu deyu gongzuo yaodian [Key issues of moral education in 2000: Guidelines from the Ministry of Education]. *Deyu Xinxi, 51* (3), 2.

Morse, J. (2003). *A level playing field: Problems in school finance* (unpublished draft).

Murr, A. (1999, May 10). Follow the firearms. *Newsweek,* p. 34.

National Commission on Excellence in Education. (1983). *A nation at risk.* Cambridge, MA: USA Research.

Nelson, J., Palonsky, S. B., & Carlson, K. (2000). *Critical issues in education: A dialectic approach* (4th ed.). New York: McGraw-Hill.

Nielsen, L. (1998). New study shows states returning to character education. *Character Educator,* (6), 9.

Noddings, N. (1984). *Caring: A feminine approach to ethics and moral education.* Berkeley, CA: University of California Press.

———. (1992). *The challenge to care in schools: An alternative approach to education.* New York: Teachers College Press.

———. (1993). *Educating for intelligent belief or unbelief.* New York: Teachers College Press.

———. (1995). *Philosophy of education.* Boulder, CO: Westview Press.

———. (2002). *Educating moral people: A caring alternative to character education.* New York: Teachers College Press.

Nucci, L. (Ed.) (1989). *Moral development and character education: A dialogue.* Berkeley, CA: McCutchan.

Pinar, W. (1994). *Autobiography, politics, and sexuality: Essays in curriculum theory 1972–1992.* New York: Peter Lang.

Ponton, L. E. (1999, May 10). Their dark romance with risk. *Newsweek*, p. 55.

Power, F. C., Higgins, A., & Kohlberg, L. (1989). *Lawrence Kohlberg's approach to moral education.* New York: Columbia University Press.

Purpel, D. (1997). The politics of character education. In A. Molnar (Ed.), *The construction of children's character* (pp. 140–153). Chicago: The University of Chicago Press.

———. (1999). The politics of character education. In D. Purpel, *Moral outrage in education* (pp. 83–97). New York: Peter Lang.

Railton, P. (2000). Morality, ideology, and reflection; or, the duck sits yet. In E. Harcourt (Ed.), *Morality, reflection, and ideology*, pp. 113–147. London: Oxford University Press.

Raths, L. E., Harmin, M., & Simon, S. B. (1966). *Values and teaching: Working with values in classroom.* Columbus, OH: Charles E. Merrill.

———. (1978). *Values and teaching: Working with values in the classroom* (second ed.). Columbus, OH: Charles E. Merrill.

Ravitch, D. (1995). *National standards in American education: A citizen's guide.* Washington, D C: Brookings Institution Press.

Rich, J. M., & DeVitis, J. L. (1992). *Competition in education.* Springfield, IL: Charles C. Thomas.

Rothstein, R. (2001, August 29). SAT scores aren't up. Not bad, not bad at all. *The New York Times*, p. B8.

Ryan, K. (1989). In defense of character education. In L. Nucci (Ed.), *Moral development and character education* (pp. 3–17). Berkeley, CA: McCutchan.

Sarri, R. (1986). Gender and race differences in criminal justice processing. *Women's Studies International Forum* (9), 89–99.

Schaps, E., Schaeffer, E. F., & McDonnell, S. N. (2001, September 12). What's right and wrong in character education today. *Education Week*, pp. 40, 44.

Scherrer, Paul. (1998, July 21). One in four US children under six live in poverty. Available at the World Socialist Web Site. Retrieved June 14, 2003, from http://www.wsws.org/news/1998/july1998/pov-j21.shtml.

Sealey, G. (2001, August 6). The noble profession: While teachers slaying are rare, the job can still be harrowing. Retrieved August 8, 2001, from http://www.abcnews.com.

Shea, C. M., Kahane, E., & Sola, P. (Eds.) (1989). *The new servants of power: A critique of the 1980s school reform movement.* Westport, CT: Greenwood Press.

Shockley, M. (2001, April 1). Why no shootings in inner-city schools? Kids' violence in the hoods takes a different form than in the burbs. *Miami Herald.*

Singer, A. (1994). Why schools should make condoms available to teenagers. *Educational Leadership, 52* (2), 78–79.

References

———. (2000). Response to Milson on character education. *Theory & Research in Social Education, 28* (2), 273–277.

Spina, S. U. (2000). Introduction: Violence in schools: Expanding the dialogue. In S. U. Spina (Ed.), *Smoke and mirrors: The hidden context of violence in schools and society* (pp. 1–39). Lanham, MD: Rowman & Littlefield.

Stedman, L. C. (1987). It's time we changed the effective schools formula. *Phi Delta Kappan, 69* (3), 215–224.

———. (1993). The condition of education: Why school reformers are on the right track. *Phi Delta Kappan, 75* (3), 215–225.

———. (1995, November 5). Putting the system to the test. *The Washington Post*, 16–17.

Stroup, F. N. (1931). Character education in Newark. *New York State Education, 18*, 571–573.

Sun, X. (2000, June). *Moral and character education in elementary and secondary schools in China.* Paper presented at the Second International Conference on Character Education, San Diego, CA.

Toppo, G. (2001, March 2). Report: Blacks three times as likely to be special ed. students. *The Associate Press State and Local Wire*, Friday, BC cycle.

The 2000 campaign; Second Presidential debate between Gov. Bush and Vice President Gore (2000, October 12). Retrieved July 15, 2002, from LEXIS-NEXIS Academic Universe.

Tyack, D. B. (1974). *The one best system: A history of American urban education.* Cambridge: Harvard University Press.

Tyack, D. B., & Cuban, L. (1995). *Tinkering toward utopia: A century of public school reform.* Cambridge: Harvard University Press.

United States Bureau of Census. (2001). *Statistical abstracts of the United States: 2001 a national data book.* Washington, DC: United States Government Printing Office.

U.S. still lags in cutting teen pregnancy. Retrieved November 29, 2001, from http://www.cnn.com.

U.S. teen pregnancy rate hit record low in 1997. Retrieved June 12, 2001, from http://www.cnn.com.

Webster's College Dictionary. (1991). New York: Random House.

Weis, L., & Fine, M. (Eds.) (1993). *Beyond silenced voices: Class, race, and gender in United States schools.* Albany, NY: State University of New York Press.

White, J. T. (1909). *Character lessons in American biography for public schools and home instruction.* New York: The Character Development League.

Wynne, E. A. (1989a). Transmitting traditional values in contemporary schools. In L. Nucci (Ed.), *Moral development and character development* (pp. 19–36). Berkeley, CA: McCutchan.

———. (1989b). Managing effective schools: The moral element. In M. Holmes, K. Leithword, & D. Musella (Eds.), *Educational policy for effective schools* (pp. 128–142). Toronto: OISE Press.

Wynne, E. A., & Ryan, K. (1997). *Reclaiming our schools: Teaching character, academics, and discipline.* Upper Saddle River, NJ: Prentice Hall.

Yuan, B., & Shen, J. (1998). Moral values held by early adolescents in Taiwan and Mainland China. *Journal of Moral Education, 27* (2), 191–207.

Yulish, S. M. (1980). *The search for a civic religion: A history of the character education movement in America, 1890–1935.* Washington, DC: University Press of America.

Zatz, M. S. (1987). The changing forms of racial/ethnic biases in sentencing. *Journal of Research in Crime and Delinquency,* (24), 69–92.

Zhan, W. (1996, June). *General trend of moral education in China in the twenty-first century.* Paper presented at the International Conference on Confucian Ethics and Eastern Culture, Beijing, China.

Index

A Nation at Risk, 59
Absolutism, 3, 45, 119, 146, 152, 154
Abstinence-based sex education, 96, 124, 126
Academic standards, 59, 91–92, 114, 117, 138, 151
Adler, Patricia A., 67, 70–71
Anyon, Jean, 22, 141
Apple, Michael, 151, 153
Aristotle, 2, 98, 106, 108, 119, 144
Authoritarianism, 141, 146, 152

"Bag of virtues," 17, 20, 51
Banks, James A., 60
Becker, Howard, 71
Behavioral training, 3, 11, 13, 16, 21, 108, 119, 134, 141, 146
Behaviorism, 146
Bennett, William J., 4, 20–21, 23, 52, 58–79, 83, 90–94, 96, 98, 103–105, 109, 111–114, 117, 119, 122–124, 129, 132, 145, 149–151
Berliner, David C., 59
Best, Joel, 67
Bloom, Allan, 60
Bowles, Samuel, 56
Bush, George, W., 3, 7, 23, 99

Cardinal Principles of Secondary Education, 39, 41
Character Education
  Association, 37
  Partnership (CEP), 115, 127, 129–130, 135, 140, 144–145, 147
Character education programs, 21, 30, 34–41, 105, 107, 130–138

Character traits, 12, 24, 34, 37–39, 41–42, 45, 77, 79, 99, 105, 107, 113, 118, 130, 136-141, 143, 150
China, 5, 8–12, 15-17, 20–22, 120,149
Chinese moral education, 5, 9, 13–14, 16–18, 20, 24
Chomsky, Noam, 85
Citizenship education, 42, 46, 99–100
Class, 1–3, 21–22, 71, 89, 108, 110, 141, 150
Classism, 5
Clinton, William. J., 3, 7, 23, 85, 99
Cognitive-developmental approach to moral education, 49–52, 55, 103–105, 154–155
Coles, Robert, 119, 121, 153
Collective education, 10
Collectivism, 10, 14
Commercialism, 83–84
Common culture, 56, 58
Common School movement, 28–29,
Communism, 14–16, 18
Communist Party, 10, 14–16, 21, 143, 149
Community
  consensus, 21, 141–142
  -based decision-making, 2, 21, 141, 143, 150
Competition, 37, 48, 57, 84, 89, 92
Comprehensive approach to character education, 111–115
Confucianism, 14–16, 18
Connell, William F., 12, 14
Conservatism, 3, 146
Cross-cultural inquiry, 7-25
Cultural diversity, 4, 49, 60, 125, 151, 156
Cultural Revolution, 11–12, 14–15

Index

Curriculum
  hidden, 18–19, 22, 24
  national, 10, 14, 16, 151

Damon, William, 2
Delpit, Lisa, 141
Democracy, 3, 24, 48, 50, 104, 123, 151
DeVitis, Joseph, 84, 92
Dewey, John, 45–46, 100, 116–117, 119–120, 153
Dogmatism, 135, 139, 146, 152
Drug abuse, 56, 60, 62–63, 69, 79–82, 93
Durkheim, Emile, 70, 98

Effective Schools, 109–110
Eleven Principles of Effective Character Education, 115, 127
Erikson, Kai, 70
Ethics of care, 154

Fine, Michelle, 74, 91, 141
"Five Loves Education," 11

Gallup polls, 22
Garbarino, James, 80, 82, 86, 93–94
Gender, 2, 21, 141, 150
Gilligan, Carol, 51
Giroux, Henry, 5, 22, 89, 95–97
Gore, Al, 23
Gun control, 86–88
Gun culture, 83, 86

Hartshorne and May Study, 46–47, 151
High-stakes testing, 7, 14, 88, 92, 138–139, 141, 151, 154–155
Holistic view of education, 115–118
Hutchins, William, 37

Ideology, 5, 7–9, 14–15, 22, 24, 103–104, 129, 133, 139
Imperialism, 84
Individualism, 15, 21, 30–31, 64, 153
Indoctrination, 21, 49, 104, 106, 125, 145–146
Internet, 81–82

Jiang, Zemin, 10, 13
Judeo-Christian ethics (values), 108–110, 122, 124, 142, 146

Katz, Michael B., 28–29
Kilpatrick, William K., 20, 64, 71, 105–108, 111–114, 118, 129, 146, 150
Kliebard, Herbert H., 39
Kohlberg, Lawrence, 50–53, 104–105, 112, 155
Kohn, Alfie, 21, 27–28, 111, 126, 129, 144, 151
Kozol, Jonathan, 78, 90, 92

Ladson-Billings, Gloria, 141
Leming, James, 20, 28, 30, 36, 65, 129–134, 139, 147, 151
Lickona, Thomas, 2, 4, 7, 19–21, 32, 55–56, 61–62, 64–67, 70–71, 79, 94, 97–99, 103, 105, 111–119, 122–126, 129, 132, 134–135, 144, 150–151
Lu, Jie, 16

Mao, Zedong (Tzetung), 11–15
Marxism, 15
McClellan, B. Edward, 27–28, 30, 36, 41, 43–45, 48–49
McGuffey readers, 29, 41
McKown, Harry, 29–32, 35–39, 42, 44
Ministry of Education, 9–11, 15
Militarism, 3, 85
Moral decline, 55–56, 95–96, 160–172
Moral development, 4, 6, 17–19, 33, 39, 50–52, 138, 141
Moral dilemmas, 52–53
Moral education
  alternative, 152–155
  virtue-centered, 118–122
Moral reasoning, 51–52
Moral training, 22, 27–31, 33–34, 41, 48, 70–72, 105, 115–117, 129, 150
Moralism, 96, 115, 118
Multiculturalism, 59–60

National Education Association (NEA), 29, 33, 38, 42, 45, 98

Index

National Rifle Association (NRA), 86–87
"National Schools of Character," 135–138
9/11, 85
Noddings, Nel, 20, 28, 52, 111, 116–117, 120, 122, 125, 129, 142–143, 151, 154–155
Nucci, Larry, 23

One-virtue-per-month approach (model), 5, 37, 137, 144, 154

Paige, Rod, 69, 87–88, 92
Patriotic education, 10
Patriotism, 10, 14, 64, 98
Pinar, William F., 57
Political control, 2, 16–17, 25, 41, 43
Political education, 10–13
Politicization, 16, 24, 55
Politics, 4–5, 7–9, 14, 22, 24–25, 152, 155–156
Popular culture, 61, 82, 84, 95
Positivism, 64
Poverty, 61, 64, 72–79, 83, 88–90, 96
   child, 88–89
   moral, 60, 63–64, 72, 74, 76–80
Power
   elites, 2, 4, 152
   relations, 6, 8, 16, 21, 98, 153
Privilege, 2, 68
Progressive education, 30
Puritan tradition (values), 33, 42, 126
Purpel, David, 1, 21, 23, 126, 152

Race, 2, 21, 74–76, 91, 141, 150
Racism, 3, 5, 64, 74–76, 80, 83, 90–91, 139, 154
Raths, Louis, 50
Ravitch, Diane, 59
"Reform and Open Door Policy," 12
Relative deprivation, 73, 89
Relativism, 49, 71, 152, 154
   moral, 2–3, 18–19, 51, 104, 110, 122
Religion, 2, 15, 18–19, 30–31, 61, 108–128, 143, 146
Restructuring of schools, 5, 154, 155
Role model, 105, 107, 127, 138, 144

Root causes, 1, 64, 73, 77, 80, 83
Ryan, Kevin, 6, 20, 22–23, 64, 99–100, 103, 111–114, 117, 129, 141, 150

Scapegoats, 95–96
Schaps, Eric, 21, 115, 144–145, 147–148
School shooting, 1, 56, 69–70, 75, 86–88
Sexism, 5
Shea, Christine M., 57
Singer, Alan, 22–23, 126
Social justice, 4, 143
Social problems, 1, 13–14, 20, 22, 32, 45, 56, 63, 72, 79, 95, 99, 115, 138, 149–150
Social transformation, 6
Socialism, 10–11, 14, 153
Socialization, 16, 20, 41, 49, 56, 95, 97–100, 152–153
Sociocultural analysis, 80
Spina, Stephanie Urso, 69, 83
Standardized testing, 4–5, 118, 145
Standards movement, 4, 138, 151–152, 155
Stedman, Lawrence, 59, 68–69
Stories (in character education), 38, 104, 107, 116

Teenage pregnancy, 66
Tracking, 90–91, 154, 156
Transformative school reform, 4, 152
2002 White House Conference on Character Education, 98
Tyack, David B., 98

U.S. foreign policy, 84–85

Values clarification, 49–52, 103–106
Violence, 6, 20, 56, 60–62, 66–67, 69, 72, 74–75, 78–95, 97–98, 120, 127, 138, 150
   school, 67, 69, 83
   socially sanctioned, 85
Virtue ethics, 2, 108, 119
Virtues, 2, 4–5, 7, 10, 14–15, 17, 19–20, 28, 30, 32, 36–38, 45, 47, 51, 103–109, 111, 113–115, 117–123, 136, 140, 142, 144–145, 150–151, 153–155

Universal, 2, 119, 150

"War on terrorism," 85
Weis, Lois, 74, 141
Well-rounded education, 13, 17, 20, 33, 39, 118–117
White House, 1, 98–99
White, James Terry, 32, 37, 150

Wynne, Edward A., 2, 4, 6, 21, 64, 71, 91, 103, 108–112, 114, 117–118, 122, 124, 129, 141–142, 145–146, 150–151

Youth deviance, 69–71, 77, 89–90, 93, 156
Yulish, Stephen M., 32–34, 36, 38, 40–44

Zero-tolerance policy, 5, 154

AC / SS — Adolescent Cultures, School & Society

Joseph L. DeVitis & Linda Irwin-DeVitis
GENERAL EDITORS

As schools struggle to redefine and restructure themselves, they need to be cognizant of the new realities of adolescents. Thus, this series of monographs and textbooks is committed to depicting the variety of adolescent cultures that exist in today's post-industrial societies. It is intended to be a primarily qualitative research, practice, and policy series devoted to contextual interpretation and analysis that encompasses a broad range of interdisciplinary critique. In addition, this series will seek to provide a pragmatic, pro-active response to the current backlash of conservatism that continues to dominate political discourse, practice, and policy. This series seeks to address issues of curriculum theory and practice; multicultural education; aggression and violence; the media and arts; school dropouts; homeless and runaway youth; alienated youth; at-risk adolescent populations; family structures and parental involvement; and race, ethnicity, class, and gender studies.

Send proposals and manuscripts to the general editors at:
> Joseph L. DeVitis & Linda Irwin-DeVitis
> College of Education and Human Development
> University of Louisville
> Louisville, KY 40292-0001

To order other books in this series, please contact our Customer Service Department at:
> (800) 770-LANG (within the U.S.)
> (212) 647-7706 (outside the U.S.)
> (212) 647-7707 FAX

or browse online by series at:
> WWW.PETERLANGUSA.COM